10|19                                                    U 15

CN

CITY AND COUNTY OF SWANSEA LIBRARIES

# A POCKET GUIDE
# TO BRITISH GALLANTRY AWARDS

# ACKNOWLEDGEMENTS

Many of the illustrations used in this work are derived from the Spink archive and from the author's own collection. Additional photographs have kindly been provided by other collectors and by courtesy of Messrs. DNW.

The author would also like to thank Emma Howard, Russell Whittle and Jack West-Sherring of Spink for their assistance and support during the production of this book.

# A POCKET GUIDE
# TO BRITISH GALLANTRY AWARDS

PETER DUCKERS

SPINK

First edition published in Great Britain
in 2019 by Spink and Son Ltd

Copyright © Peter Duckers, 2019

A CIP catalogue record for this book is available from
the British Library

ISBN 978-1-912667-02-4
Typeset by Russ Whittle

Printed and bound in Malta by Gutenberg Press

Spink and Son Ltd
69 Southampton Row
London WC1B 4ET

www.spinkbooks.com

# CONTENTS

*An example of a Civil War 'Royalist Reward'. Some awards were given for gallantry by both sides of the conflict but original examples of all types are now very rare.*

# INTRODUCTION

Since the days of the earliest organised states, gallantry in battle has been highly regarded and often highly rewarded. Over the years, different societies have rewarded gallantry in a variety of ways – examples being elevation in rank or status, awards of land, grants of money, jewels, presentation weapons or clothing or other valuable gifts reflecting that particular society's estimation of the significance of the action.

The idea of awarding wearable medals for bravery certainly goes back to antiquity and at least to Roman times – soldiers wearing circular or half-circular badges of merit on their armour are seen on military gravestones. Medals for gallantry were first awarded in any number in England during the Civil Wars of 1642-51, when the King and individual commanders on both sides presented such rewards to their own men. Examples are the two gold medals awarded by the King to Robert Welch and John Smith for their conspicuous gallantry in saving the royal standard at Edgehill in 1642. Such medals were given only in small numbers and few survive, so that examples are rare and valuable.

In the late seventeenth century, the introduction of official Naval Rewards under Charles II for service in the various Dutch Wars seems to have heralded the beginning of a regulated, national system of gallantry awards, but in fact nothing developed from it and throughout the eighteenth century medals for bravery were conferred in a fairly *ad hoc* manner. Decorations for gallantry in action were presented occasionally by the monarch or by individual patrons, colleagues or even societies, but there was no standardised national system – the medals were produced in a variety of forms and metals as and when required and in small numbers.

During the long French Revolutionary and Napoleonic Wars of 1793-1815, this absence of a formal system of reward was

*The Naval Reward of 1665, awarded for combat in the Dutch Wars.*

clearly noticed – some regiments began to produce their own distinctive medals to officers and men singled out for gallant conduct. A wide range of attractive and interesting medals was the result, but many regiments and corps never produced such awards and again they tended to be issued only in small numbers and can be rare. The Naval Gold Medals of 1793-1815 and the Army Gold Crosses and Gold Medals of 1808-1814

*Examples of regimentally produced medals for the Peninsular War – to recipients in the 74th Foot and the 23rd Light Dragoons. There are many different types.*

could be awarded for gallant conduct but tended to reward leadership and distinguished service rather than specific acts of gallantry; they were only granted to officers and only a small number was ever issued. As a general principle, the monarch and the state did not recognise in any formal medallic manner the gallantry of their own forces.

This situation prevailed until the Russian War of 1854-56. Acts of gallantry by British naval and military forces in the Baltic

*The Army Gold Cross – the Cross reflected four distinct awards. Further actions were rewarded with large, solid gold bars bearing the name of the battle, carried on the ribbon. All are exceptionally rare.*

*The Army Gold Medal. The name of the initial battle for which the award was made (in this case Vittoria in 1813) is carried on the reverse; gold bars commemorated further awards (in this example for Orthes in southern France).*

and, in particular, in the Crimea, were brought to the attention of the wider public via regular newspaper reports from the seat of war. The result was the demand for the creation of a national system of honours with which to reward British forces on active service.

From this arose the institution of the Distinguished Conduct Medal (DCM) in December 1854, followed by the Conspicuous Gallantry Medal (CGM) in September 1855. The former was solely awarded to NCOs and 'Other Ranks' of the British army and the latter to the 'Other Ranks' and ratings of the Royal Marines and Royal Navy. Despite the creation of these two new decorations, it was nevertheless considered that there was still a gap in the system – there was, for example, no gallantry award for officers apart from the rather grand Order of the Bath, which did not, in any case, tend to be conferred for gallantry in one action. The result was the introduction in January 1856 of the Victoria Cross, made retrospective to the beginning of the Russian War. The award was unusual in its day in being available to all personnel of Britain's armed forces, regardless

*The Russian War 1854-56: the fighting in the Crimea led to the creation of the first national system of gallantry awards.*

of rank or status, in one form, without grades or classes and in one metal (bronze). It was a very plain, simple-looking medal but it came to represent the highest gallantry in action and it remains the most senior gallantry award in the British system.

Since 1856, the British honours system has been extended as and when necessary, with major wars often being the spur to the creation of additional types of decoration and a major reform in 1993 considerably simplifying the whole structure. Also, increasingly since the Second World War, most Commonwealth Dominions and countries have established their own series of awards and decorations which they confer rather than relying on those emanating from the British system.

The work which follows offers a succinct overview, with examples, of the main awards to British, Imperial and Commonwealth personnel of all branches of the armed services to reward their gallantry in action.

# BRITISH MILITARY AWARDS FOR GALLANTRY LISTED IN ORDER OF PRECEDENCE, WITH DATES OF INSTITUTION AND, WHERE APPLICABLE, OBSOLESCENCE

| | |
|---|---|
| The Victoria Cross | (1856) |
| The George Cross | (1940) |
| The Conspicuous Gallantry Cross | (1993) |
| The Distinguished Service Order | (1886) |
| The Indian Order of Merit | (1837 - 1947) |
| The Distinguished Service Cross | (1914) |
| The Military Cross | (1914) |
| The Distinguished Flying Cross | (1918) |
| The Air Force Cross | (1918) |
| The Distinguished Conduct Medal | (1854 - 1993) |
| The Conspicuous Gallantry Medal | (1855/1874 - 1993) |
| The Conspicuous Gallantry Medal (Flying) | (1942 - 1993) |
| The George Medal | (1940) |
| The Indian Distinguished Service Medal | (1907 - 1947) |
| The Distinguished Service Medal | (1914 - 1993) |
| The Military Medal | (1916 - 1993) |
| The Distinguished Flying Medal | (1918 - 1993) |
| The Air Force Medal | (1918 - 1993) |
| The Burma Gallantry Medal | (1942 - 1948) |
| The Queen's Gallantry Medal | (1974) |
| The British Empire Medal for Gallantry | (1922 - 1974) |
| The Meritorious Service Medal for Gallantry | (1916 - 1928) |

# THE VICTORIA CROSS

The Victoria Cross was and remains the highest decoration for gallantry conferred in Britain, the Empire and Commonwealth. It was another award born out of the conditions of the Russian War of 1854-56, which had already seen the creation of the Distinguished Conduct Medal (for the Army) and the Conspicuous Gallantry Medal (for the Royal Navy and Royal Marines). But neither of these was available to officers and it was still felt that there was a need for another, higher level reward for outstanding gallantry. The result – with the active involvement of the Queen and Prince Albert throughout the design process – was the institution of the Victoria Cross in January 1856.

*The Victoria Cross. The bronze is hand chased and chemically blackened to give a dark finish. This is a Victorian example.*

It was to be awarded for 'most conspicuous bravery, or some daring or pre-eminent act of valour or self-sacrifice, or extreme devotion to duty in the presence of the enemy'; awards for gallantry not in the face of the enemy – six of which were conferred – effectively ceased in 1881.

*Obverse and Reverse of the Victoria Cross – in this case an award for 1914.*

The decoration takes the form of a chemically darkened bronze cross *pattée* (not, as often stated, a Maltese cross), bearing the St. Edward crown surmounted by a lion, above the inscription FOR VALOUR. This was chosen by Queen Victoria from a range of suggested legends. Each medal is hand finished, so that slight detail differences may be visible from one to the other. The cross is suspended by a ring from a seriffed 'V' to a laurelled bar through which the ribbon passes.

Manufactured since its foundation by the London jewellers, Messrs. Hancocks, the VC carries the name and unit details of the recipient engraved on the reverse of the suspension bar and the date or dates of the deed for which the award is made in the central roundel on the reverse. Initially, awards to the Royal Navy and Royal Marines were carried from a plain, dark blue ribbon and those to the army from plain crimson ('red'); these were standardised to the crimson type in 1918 (formally in 1920). Since 1917, a small miniature VC is carried in the centre of the ribbon strip when ribbons alone are worn.

*The VC with blue ribbon as originally worn by RN and RM recipients.*

*The reverse of a Victoria Cross, showing typical engraved naming location and style. The award to Gunner James Park of the Bengal Artillery for gallantry in the relief of Lucknow in November 1857. Park died of disease before he could actually wear the medal.*

*Since 1917, when ribbons alone are worn, a small replica of the award is carried on the ribbon.*

Unusually for its day and considering its intended significance, the medal was conferred in only one class, regardless of the rank or status of the recipient, and was worked in plain bronze, not in elaborate enamels or bullion metal. The 'tuppence worth of bronze' was intended to signify the highest gallantry without being a decorative jewel. From 1898, a special annual pension was paid to recipients; this currently stands at a tax-free £10,000 per annum, raised in 2015 from £2,129.

The first awards of the new medal, which was made retrospective to the beginning of the Russian War in February 1854, were gazetted on 24th February 1857, the first chronologically being to Mate C. D. Lucas, awarded the decoration for his gallantry in throwing overboard a live shell which had landed on the deck of HMS *Hecla* in action in the Baltic on 21st June 1854. The first award to be actually gazetted was that to Lt. C. W. Buckley, R.N., for gallantry in the Sea of Azoff in 1855 and the first examples to be personally presented by the Queen were given in a grand ceremony in Hyde Park on 26th June 1857. On that occasion, no fewer than 62 (out of 111) VCs for the Russian War were given to their recipients,

*The VC with DSO and campaign medals awarded to Lieut. (later Lieut. Col.)*
*W. G. Cubitt (1835-1903), 13th Bengal Infantry. VC awarded for gallantry*
*in saving three wounded men in the action at Chinhut, defence of Lucknow, in*
*June 1857. Later awarded the DSO for Burma 1885-87. Sold at Spink in April*
*2018 for £216,000.*

the first person to actually receive the new medal being Lt. Henry Raby R.N., earned for his gallantry at Sebastopol in the Crimea. VCs have been awarded to fathers and sons and to brothers; the youngest recipient is believed to have been the fifteen-year old Hospital Apprentice A. Fitzgibbon (China 1860) and the oldest the 69-year old Captain W. Raynor of the Bengal Veteran Establishment (Delhi, 1857). It has not yet been awarded to a woman. The most VCs awarded for one day of action was 23 for Lucknow on 16th November 1857, 12 for the battle of Inkermann in the Crimea on 5th November 1854 and 11 for the defence of Rorke's Drift in the Zulu War on 22nd/23rd January 1879.

Bars were sanctioned for the VC to cater for further awards of the decoration to the same recipient, but to date only three have been conferred – to Surgeon A. Major Martin-Leake (South Africa 1902 and France 1914), posthumously to Captain Noel Chevasse MC (Western Front 1916 and 1917) and to the New Zealander, Captain Charles Upham (Crete 1941 and North Africa 1942).

Since 1855, 1358, according to David Erskine-Hill. This includes the three bars to Victoria Crosses. VCs have been awarded, its scope extended by amendment to its warrants over the years e.g. to 'local forces' (such as colonial militias) in 1867, to the Indian Army in 1911, to the Merchant Navy and to aerial forces in 1920. Posthumous awards were first made in 1902 – when some for the Zulu War of 1879 were presented to next-of-kin – and officially as of 1907, and the forfeiture of the decoration for dishonourable conduct was effectively ended by order of King George V after World War I, with the names of eight 'forfeited' VCs being restored to the register of the award.

*A miniature of the VC. Miniature awards of the VC (and other decorations and medals) were worn in mess kit or in less formal dress. They were privately purchased and vary greatly in the quality of their workmanship.*

Early (pre-1914) awards tend to carry only very bland citations – though with the VC there is generally little difficulty in establishing the action of the recipient in greater detail by referring to regimental or unit histories, biographies, obituaries, newspaper reports etc. A typical example is the VC awarded to Robert Newell of the 9th Lancers for his action in the final recapture of Lucknow in 1858, one of no fewer than 182 awarded for the Indian Mutiny. Its brief citation, based on the dispatch of the cavalry commander Sir James Hope Grant, was published on 24th December 1858:

> 'On 19th March 1858, during the assault on the city of Lucknow, Private Newell went to the assistance of a comrade whose horse had stumbled and fallen on the rocky ground. Newell raced over, and managed to bring the man to safety, under the heavy musket fire from the rebels.'

Newell would not live to see the VC; soon after his action at Lucknow, he died of dysentery on 11th July 1858 at Umballa and was buried in an unmarked grave in the cemetery there. His medals were given to his widow and are now in Lord Ashcroft's collection.

Colonial conflicts large and small naturally saw varying numbers of VC awards – as examples, 15 for the Maori Wars, 1860-66, 23 for the Zulu War of 1879, 16 for the Afghan War of 1878-80, five for the Sudan 1884-85, 11 for the North West Frontier 1897-98 and 78 for the larger South African (Boer) War of 1899-1902.

Much more detail on the circumstances of individual awards appears in those conferred for 1914-18 and later, and leads to the inevitable conclusion that the gallantry required to win the VC reached almost unattainable heights as time passed.

Of the 628 awards for WWI, an outstanding example was that to the Canadian pilot William George Barker VC, DSO and Bar, MC and Bar – an 'Ace' with a truly remarkable record of air combat and gallantry even before he was awarded the VC in 1918. On 27th October 1918, Barker left his airbase at La Targette in a Snipe aircraft, ordered to return it to Hounslow

*The Second China War VC and group of medals awarded to Major-General R. M. Rogers, 44th Foot; during the attack on the North Taku Fort in 1860, Rogers swam the ditches and was the first man to enter the enemy fortress, receiving severe wounds.*

and choosing to fly back along the Front. When over enemy lines above the Forêt de Mormal, he attacked an enemy two-seater which broke up, its crew escaping by parachute. He was then caught ('bounced') by a formation of Fokker DVIIs of *Jagdgruppe* 12. Nothing daunted, and deciding that attack was one form of defence, he single-handedly took on more than fifteen enemy aircraft, being wounded three times in the legs and having his left elbow blown away. Nevertheless, he managed to retain control of his plane and bring down three more enemy aircraft in a dogfight which took place over the lines of the Canadian Corps. Severely wounded and bleeding badly, Barker force-landed his Snipe inside Allied lines, his life being saved by the men of an RAF Balloon Section, who took him to a dressing station. Transferred to the General Hospital at Rouen, he lay unconscious for days and awoke to the news that he was to receive the Victoria Cross.

His VC was officially gazetted on 30th November 1918 and on 1st March 1919 Barker, with one arm still in a sling, and hobbling on a walking stick, was invested with his many decorations by the King in one ceremony at Buckingham

Palace. Sad to say, after working in the civil air service after the war, he was killed in a flying accident in Canada in 1930; his VC and other decorations and medals are now displayed in the Canadian War Museum in Ottawa.

*The VC group to Corporal C. Barron, 3rd Canadian Infantry, for gallantry at Passchendaele in 1917; during the attack on 'Vine Cottage' on 6 November, Barron single-handedly cleared three enemy machine-gun posts, enabling the position to be taken.*

181 VCs and one Bar were conferred for World War II. One which demonstrates the extremes of gallantry necessary to earn 'the Cross' was that conferred posthumously on Captain J. N. Randle of the 2nd Royal Norfolk Regiment for his incredible gallantry and personal sacrifice at Kohima in May 1944. The citation from *The London Gazette* reads:

'On the 4th May, 1944, at Kohima in Assam, a Battalion of the Royal Norfolk Regiment attacked the Japanese positions on a nearby ridge. Captain Randle took over command of the Company which was leading the attack when the Company Commander was severely wounded. His handling of a difficult situation in the face of heavy fire was masterly and although wounded himself in the knee by grenade splinters he continued to inspire his men by his initiative, courage and outstanding leadership until the Company had captured its objective and consolidated its position. He then went forward and brought in all the wounded men who were lying outside the perimeter. In spite of his painful wound Captain Randle refused to be evacuated and insisted on carrying out a personal reconnaissance with great daring in bright moonlight prior to a further attack by his Company on the position to which the enemy had withdrawn. At dawn on 6th May the attack opened, led by Captain Randle, and one of the platoons succeeded in reaching the crest of the hill held by the Japanese. Another platoon, however, ran into heavy medium machine gun fire from a bunker on the reverse slope of the feature.

Captain Randle immediately appreciated that this particular bunker covered not only the rear of his new position but also the line of communication of the battalion so that the destruction of the enemy post was imperative if the operation were to succeed. With utter disregard of the obvious danger

*The posthumous VC and campaign medals to Wing Commander H. G. Malcolm (1917-42), 18 Squadron RAF. For gallantry in leading Blenheim bombers in attacks on heavily-defended targets in Tunisia, during which he was killed.*

to himself Captain Randle charged the Japanese machine gun post single-handed with rifle and bayonet. Although bleeding in the face and mortally wounded by numerous bursts of machine gun fire he reached the bunker and silenced the gun with a grenade thrown through the bunker slit. He then flung his body across the slit so that the aperture should be completely sealed. The bravery shown by this officer could not have been surpassed and by his self-sacrifice he saved the lives of many of his men and enabled not only his own Company but the whole Battalion to gain its objective and win a decisive victory over the enemy.'

Quite fittingly, Randle's VC is now displayed in the Imperial War Museum.

More recently, Australia, New Zealand (both in 1991) and Canada (in 1993) have established their own version of the VC i.e. one which they award as a national decoration without requiring the sanction of the 'home' authorities but retaining the historic title. It remains the same in all respects regarding its status and design, the only variation being that the Canadian version now carries the legend *Pro Valore* in place of the original *For Valour*, to respect the sentiments of French-speaking Canadians. To date, no Canadian Victoria Cross has been awarded but four Australian and one New Zealand type have been conferred.

*A recent replica of the VC produced by Messrs. Hancocks, the makers of the award since its institution. These were produced to celebrate the 150th Anniversary of the VC in 2007 and were cast from the original dies.*

# THE GEORGE CROSS

By the beginning of the Second World War, there was a complex and potentially confusing array of medals available to reward civilian gallantry. These ranged from high-ranking official awards (like the venerable Albert Medal, the Empire Gallantry Medal, the Edward Medals for mines and industry, the Sea Gallantry Medal and others), to society and local medals like those awarded by the Royal Humane Society and Liverpool Shipwreck and Humane Society.

Nevertheless, the onset of 'The Blitz' and the mass air bombing of Britain brought to attention the potential need for a high-ranking national reward for bravery. The result was the creation in 1940 of the George Cross and the George Medal.

*The London Blitz – acts of gallantry shown in this and air attacks on other British cities and ports led to the creation of the George Cross and George Medal.*

The George Cross (GC) – often thought of as 'the civilian VC' – was instituted by Royal Warrant of 24th September 1940 and notified in *The London Gazette* of 31st January 1941. It was to be the highest ranking civilian award for gallantry, granted for 'acts of the greatest heroism or of the most conspicuous courage in circumstances of extreme danger' and the required standard of bravery was exceptionally high. The Cross could be conferred on British and Commonwealth civilian men or women and members of the Police forces, rescue services (like fire and ambulance) and civil defence personnel. Members of the armed forces were also eligible, the award generally given, according to the original Statutes, 'for actions for which purely military Honours are not normally granted' – i.e. for actions other than in combat or 'before the enemy', like saving lives on a minefield or in bomb and mine disposal.

The most unusual awards are those to the island of Malta, conferred in 1942 to reward the fortitude of its entire civilian population during relentless German attacks, and as a collective award to the Royal Ulster Constabulary in 1999 for their years of dedicated and courageous service.

The George Cross superseded the Empire Gallantry Medal (qv) whose wearers were invited to exchange their original medal for the Cross and in 1971 the same invitation was extended to surviving holders of the Albert Medal and Edward Medals, which then became obsolete. Since only approx. 160 have so far been awarded, with only 59 after 1947, some being exchanges for the Empire Gallantry Medal, examples of the George Cross are rarely seen. Only four have been conferred on women and many recent awards have been posthumous. Bars were authorised for subsequent actions, but none has yet been conferred. Recipients now receive a tax-free gratuity of £10,000 per annum.

The decoration takes the form of a Greek cross in silver, with a narrow border, bearing a central medallion depicting St. George and the Dragon, around which are the words FOR GALLANTRY. In the angle of each arm of the cross is the royal cypher GVI. The reverse is plain but carries the name of the recipient engraved in upright capitals, with rank or branch

*The obverse of the George Cross.*     *The reverse of the decoration.*

*George Cross to Asst. Surgeon G. D. Rodrigues of the Indian Medical Service; a 1926 Empire Gallantry Medal exchanged for a George Cross.*

of service if appropriate and date of award as published in
*The London Gazette* – not the date of the incident for which
the award is made, except in the case of EGM exchanges. The
medal hangs from a straight laurelled bar via a small ring. The
ribbon is plain dark blue, carrying in the centre a miniature of
the Cross when ribbons alone are worn; ladies wear the cross
from a bow of the ribbon.

*The GC ribbon with miniature emblem.*

*The GC as worn by female recipients, of which there have been only four to date.*

As with all other gallantry awards, each incident for which
the George Cross was awarded is peculiar to that event and
recipient and generalisations are not really possible. The
example below – to Sergt. Michael Gibson, of No. 9 Bomb
Disposal Company, Royal Engineers, for the Coventry 'Blitz' –
gives a flavour of the type of action the GC was designed to
reward. Approved just twelve days after the George Cross was
instituted and published in *The London Gazette* on 21st January

1941, the decoration was awarded for 'most conspicuous gallantry in carrying out hazardous work in a very brave manner.' The original recommendation offers greater detail:

> 'On 14th September 1940 a large unexploded bomb fell in an important factory [in Coventry]. Excavation supervised by Sgt. Gibson was begun, during which time another bomb which had dropped nearby exploded. Despite the knowledge that the bomb on which he was engaged was of a similar type the N.C.O persevered and eventually the bomb was uncovered. On uncovering it an unusual hissing noise was heard coming from the bomb, whereupon Sergeant Gibson sent his men away and immediately set to work on the fuse. This he extracted safely and the bomb was eventually removed. His prompt and courageous action saved a very dangerous situation.'

Regrettably, Gibson was killed just over a month later when another unexploded bomb killed him and the entire RE section working with him.

The George Cross continues to be available to reward the highest examples of civilian and other gallantry; many later awards have been posthumous.

*The George Cross and WWII medals to Sgt. George Gibson, RE, for bomb disposal work during the Coventry Blitz.*

# THE CONSPICUOUS GALLANTRY CROSS

On several occasions during the twentieth century there had been suggestions that an increasingly complex system of bravery and gallantry awards should be simplified and reformed, especially to remove the distinction between officers and other ranks in terms of decorations. Though generally blocked by hard-line opponents of such changes, the system was finally subjected to a sweeping reform under John Major as Prime Minister in the 1990s.

The reforms removed the distinction between awards for officers and other ranks, abolishing *medals* for gallantry (like the DCM, CGM, MM, DSM, DFM and AFM) and opening the former officers' awards in the form of Crosses to all ranks (MC, DSC, DFC, AFC). Another result was the creation in October 1993 of a new high-level gallantry decoration in the form of the Conspicuous Gallantry Cross (CGC).

The CGC was conferred 'in recognition of an act or acts of conspicuous gallantry during active operations against the enemy'. It effectively replaced both the Distinguished Conduct Medal (for the Army) and the Conspicuous Gallantry Medal (for Naval, Royal Marine and Air Forces) as a 'second level' award to Other Ranks and ratings. The CGC also replaced the Distinguished Service Order (DSO) as an award to officers for gallantry. The DSO was, however, retained as an award for outstanding leadership, open to all ranks and services.

The new medal, a 'classless' award which was to rank next below the Victoria Cross, takes the form of a silver cross *pattée*, the arms joined by sprays of laurel, with a depiction of St. Edward's crown in a central roundel. The reverse is plain except for the engraving of the rank, name and unit of its recipient along with the date of award. The cross hangs via a small ring to a plain silver Bar. The ribbon is white with blue edges and a central stripe of red.

*The Conspicuous Gallantry Cross, obverse. The reverse is plain except for the recipient's details which are laser engraved.*

*The CGC with current Operational Service Medal with clasp for service in Afghanistan.*

The first awards of the CGC were made in 1995 for gallantry in Bosnia in 1994-96, in 'former Yugoslavia', during the Balkan Civil Wars of that period. Bars were authorised but none has so far been awarded.

As with other high-ranking gallantry awards, it is difficult to generalise on the nature of an action which will win the Cross. One example is that conferred on Colour Sergeant A. G. Dennis of the 2nd Battalion, The Mercian Regiment (Worcestershire & Sherwood Foresters), who, despite having been severely wounded by a roadside bomb in Helmand on his first tour of Afghanistan in 2007, returned to Afghanistan in 2009, where he was again wounded by a rocket-propelled grenade during a protracted firefight. In spite of his wounds, he continued to fire his rifle with one arm and was the last to leave the fire position, refusing medical aid. The official recommendation recorded:

'Sergt. Dennis was second in command of an Operational Mentoring and Liaison Team which was deployed to conduct a joint patrol with [Afghan soldiers] of the Afghanistan National Army [ANA]. Whilst patrolling the Helmand River

Valley they were ambushed by small arms fire and rocket propelled grenades. Dennis found himself with three other British soldiers and half of the ANA returning fire, before ordering them to break into a compound to establish a fire support position. Looking around, Dennis realised that the ANA were close to breaking and without hesitation he ran into the area of conflict and grabbed an ANA Warrior, propelling him to a safe position before repeating this action for a second time.

On the third run, he heard a 'whoosh' and turned as a RPG [rocket-propelled grenade] exploded three metres in front of him. Although the fragmentation missed him, Dennis was hurled through the air by the blast and into a ditch. For a few seconds he was unconscious and when he came to his left arm hung uselessly by his side and he was in intense pain. Undeterred, Dennis fought on, moving back to the fire support position where he used a radio to send a contact report.

The enemy then attempted to outflank the position and Dennis spotting the movement organised a counter-attack. As enemy pressure mounted Dennis fired his rifle with his one good arm whilst attempting to re-establish contact with the

*CGC awarded for Iraq, in a group with campaign awards for Northern Ireland, Afghanistan and Iraq.*

other half of his unit. Dennis was last to leave the fire support position and refused morphine so as not to dull his senses, or create a burden for his team. At the Patrol Base he refused treatment until all soldiers were safely inside and accounted for. Dennis's fighting spirit when severely wounded was outstanding and inspired others. His example and initiative brought the ANA into the battle which saved the patrol from defeat. He was calm and collected under intense fire, displaying cool courage.'

To date, approximately 60 CGCs have been conferred, some posthumously. Apart from the Unit Award to the Royal Ulster Constabulary in 2006, there were two awards for Bosnia (1995 and 1996), 11 for the various Iraq operations, about 45 awards for recent operations in Afghanistan (2002-2014) and two for actions in Sierra Leone in 2001.

One recent Afghan award went to Lieutenant Simon Cupples, The Mercian Regiment, who received the Conspicuous Gallantry Cross for bravery in Helmand, when he went back into a 'killing zone' six times through the night in an attempt to rescue wounded soldiers. Almost a third of his platoon had been shot when a force of thirty Taliban ambushed them from 20 yards. The citation recounted that:

> 'For the fifth time, he crawled forward in an attempt to recover the last casualty but the remorseless intensity of the enemy fire forced him to withdraw .... He was utterly determined not to leave his soldier behind and subsequently commanded a rescue team who successfully recovered the soldier.'

Unsurprisingly, examples of the CGC rarely occur on the market.

# THE DISTINGUISHED SERVICE ORDER

By the late nineteenth century, apart from the Victoria Cross and promotions within the Order of the Bath (which were not commonly made for a single act of gallantry) there was no reward which could be conferred on the Officers of British and Imperial armed forces for gallantry on campaign or for exceptionally meritorious service on active operations.

As a result, the Distinguished Service Order (DSO) was instituted by Royal Warrant of 6th September 1886, published in *The London Gazette* on 9th November. It is rather strangely named; describing itself as an 'Order', recipients were (at least early on) referred to as 'Companions of the DSO', but it had only one grade and one division (military) and none of the usual trappings of a formal Order – a hierarchy of grades, a chapel, dedicated officials, distinctive robes etc.

The decoration was intended to reward junior officers (below Major or 'Field Officer' rank) for services for which the Victoria Cross or grades of the Order of the Bath would not be appropriate. Initially, 'members' had to have been Mentioned in Dispatches and because the original warrant stated that the DSO was to reward 'individual instances of meritorious or distinguished service in war', many came to be conferred for generally meritorious service, sometimes over a longer period, rather than for specific acts of gallantry. This caused strong feelings, especially in World War I, so it was ordered in January 1917 that in future all awards would be for gallantry in action and to the

*The standard obverse of the DSO; slight variations in the detail of the crown are found.*

'fighting services' i.e. not for service like staff work behind the lines. The idea of having a two-tier system, with one ribbon for 'combatant' awards and one for 'non-combatant' was discussed in 1917 and 1918 but never adopted.

The DSO was made available to Army, Royal Navy, Royal Marines, Indian and Colonial officers, extended in 1918 to the Royal Air Force and in 1943 to the Merchant Navy and Home Guard. Bars to reward further acts were authorised on 23rd August 1916; these are plain silver slip-on types, with a small central crown.

*DSO with second award Bar.*       *DSO with two additional Bars.*

The obverse of the badge comprises a gold-edged cross, with concave arms, enamelled white, with a green central wreath of laurel enclosing the Imperial Crown on a red enamel background. The reverse has, in the centre of the design, the cypher of the reigning monarch below a crown, within a green wreath of laurel on a red enamel background. It is suspended from a straight laurelled bar by a narrow ribbon of red flanked by narrow blue stripes and has an integral laurelled brooch Bar for wearing.

From 1886-1887, the badge was worked in actual gold and enamel but from 1888, on the grounds of cost, it was reduced to silver-gilt except for the laurels and centre pieces. Only about 150 of the original gold type were awarded, these largely for service on the Egypt/Sudan border (e.g. for Ginnis, Sarras and Toski) and in the conquest of Upper Burma. The early awards tend to be noticeably thinner and slightly smaller.

Slight variations in design (e.g. of the central crown) can be found over the years, with various alterations to the royal cypher; in 1949, for example, a 'second type' George VI cypher was introduced, replacing the previous 'GRI' with 'GVIR', reflecting the loss of the Indian Empire in 1947.

*The reverse of the George VI award – first type (1937-47) with **GRI** monogram reflecting the King's status as Emperor of India. This was altered in 1947 with Indian independence.*

Just over 1,600 DSOs were awarded under Queen Victoria, of which the large number of 1,143 was granted for service in the Boer War (1899-1902). Only 77 awards were made under Edward VII, bearing his cypher, mainly for Somaliland and the North West Frontier of India. The figures are unsurprisingly much larger for the First World War. About 9,000 DSOs were conferred on Army officers in World War I (including later Russian operations and the Iraq campaign into 1920), with about 700 first Bars and 70 second award Bars; the most awarded to one recipient was the DSO with three Bars, of which only seven are known. Naval forces received just over 800 awards, with 52 first Bars and four second Bars; aerial forces received 61 DSOs and eight Bars. This gives a grand total in the region of 10,700 for the period 1914-1920.

*A DSO with the standard medals for the Boer War (1899-1902).*

In the interwar years, the DSO was awarded in reasonable numbers for campaigns like the Third Afghan War of 1919 (15), for operations in Waziristan and elsewhere on the North West Frontier (about 70), for Kurdistan, Burma and Palestine. For World War II, nearly 5,000 initial awards were made amongst all services, with about 500 first Bars, 60 second Bars and eight third Bars.

As usual with British decorations, the fact of an award is published in *The London Gazette* and other official journals, but in general

*Lieut. L. G. Hawker, RE and RFC, wins the DSO for bombing the German air base at Gontrode, in April 1915, shielding his attack by using a German balloon for cover.*

citations for awards prior to the First World War are very brief and lack detail. Because of its shape, it was difficult to name the award, but they are sometimes found with details privately engraved along the narrow edges of the arms or reverse of the suspension bar or brooch. From *c.* 1938 the date of award was engraved on the back of the suspension bar and on the reverse of any further award Bar. Silver rosettes (one for each Bar) were worn on the DSO ribbon if ribbons alone were being worn.

In terms of published citations, the pre 1914 awards of the DSO often carry little more than a bald statement that the decoration is awarded 'for distinguished service [or in recognition of service] in recent operations in ...' with little else. A slightly fuller example is that for the DSO awarded to Captain H. P. Airey, where the *Gazette* records its award 'for distinguished service, coolness under fire and marked gallantry' during the campaign in Burma 1885-87. It is, of course, often possible to find more about the action from regimental histories, newspaper accounts, obituaries, biographies etc.

During World War I more detail began to appear in *The London Gazette* – usually an initial announcement of the fact

*A WWI DSO with Military Cross, 1914 medal group and India General Service Medal.*

of an award followed some time later by the details. As an example, the award of the DSO to Major Harry Roberts M.C., 2nd Sussex Regiment was announced in *The London Gazette* of 15th February 1919, the unusually detailed and fine citation following on 30th July:

> 'During the operations north of Gricourt on 24th September 1918 he commanded the right front company of the battalion in the attack. After reaching the final objective and while the company was still somewhat disorganised from the attack, the enemy launched a counter-attack with about 400 men against the position occupied by his men. He was out in front of the position when the counter-attack was first seen. He returned to his company and ordered his men to open fire on the advancing enemy. As soon as he saw the first wave of the enemy wavering, he again blew his whistle and ordered the whole of the men in that area to fix bayonets and advance against the advancing enemy. The total number of men at his disposal did not exceed 80. By this action he completely routed the counter-attacking enemy and captured many prisoners. Throughout this operation he was walking about fully exposed and by his calm handling of the situation and selecting the moment to dash out against the enemy with the bayonet, was responsible for the thorough routing of a strong counter-attack and enabling the ground gained in the initial attack to be retained. During the attack he was severely wounded in the arm by a bullet fired at point-blank range but in spite of this he remained with his company, reorganising his men in defensive position and before being evacuated gave a full report of the situation to the battalion commander.'

Of course, DSOs were conferred on recipients in all services. That to Engineer Commander A. D. Merriman (*London Gazette* 14th October 1941) was awarded, according to the *Gazette,*

'For mastery, determination and skill in action against the German Battleship Bismarck.'

For this famous naval action against one of the biggest German threats to Britain's command of the sea, 15 DSOs and one Bar were awarded to officers of the Royal Navy and Fleet Air Arm, of which no fewer than seven went to Engineer Officers of various ships – reflecting the importance of maintaining the efficiency of the ships' engines and equipment on active service. The more detailed official recommendation states:

> 'HMS *Suffolk* – Engineer Officer – steamed the ship economically and efficiently at high speed throughout the [Bismarck] operations, overcoming a number of material difficulties which were the legacy of damage done to the ship during the bombardment last year and her long subsequent period lying awaiting repair.'

It was said of HMS *Suffolk* (whose commanding officer Captain R. M. Ellis, also received the DSO for the same operations), not only that 'the work of this ship was incomparable ... [she] was ... responsible for the first sighting but she remained in touch continuously until the engagement with the Battle Cruiser Force. The way in which touch was maintained under extremely difficult conditions of low and varying visibility was beyond praise.'

One award for Italy, published in *The London Gazette* of 24th January 1946, went to Lt. Colonel (later Brigadier General) C. A. Richardson of the 14th Canadian Armoured Regiment, and was announced simply as being 'In recognition of gallant and distinguished services in Italy.' By the time of his award for Italy in 1944, Richardson had already served in the Dieppe Raid in August 1942 and in the invasion of Sicily in 1943 and was second-in-command of his regiment.

As usual, the actual recommendation upon which the award was based offers much more detail and is fairly typical in explaining the gallantry, arduous service and continuous dedication to duty which went into earning the DSO during World War II:

'This officer has commanded 14 Canadian Armoured Regiment (The Calgary Regiment) since June 1944. During his term of command his regiment has been almost constantly in action, and has never failed to reach and hold its objectives. The unvarying success of the regiment has in a large measure been due to the magnificent leadership and example of Lieutenant-Colonel Richardson. Before every action he invariably conducted reconnaissance personally, both by day and by night, often under heavy and accurate mortar and shell fire. During the rapid pursuit of the enemy forces north of Lake Trasimeno, Italy, between 1st and 4th July 1944, this officer moved with the most forward troops, and by his personal example and skilful direction enabled our pursuing forces to maintain contact, thus preventing the enemy from reorganising and re-establishing a defensive line. Under heavy fire of all natures he personally directed his Reconnaissance Troop on 2nd and 3rd July 1944, seizing three bridges over

*A WWII group, with DSO for North West Europe.*

the Chiana Canal before these could be blown by the enemy, thus enabling the momentum of the advance to be continued. During the pursuit to the Arno River, on many occasions, he personally reconnaissanced [sic] routes of advance under mortar and shell fire enabling his tanks to cross country considered impassable for tanks, continuously surprising the enemy in this manner. Again during the fighting through the Gothic Line and the Apennines his personal reconnaissance, forward of the forward defended localities in heavily mined country, enabled his regiment to get forward in most difficult terrain and render support to the infantry of 8 Indian Division which resulted in the taking of many difficult features including San Bartolo Monte Carolino and Monte Budrialto. This officer's contempt of danger, personal fighting spirit, magnificent example and outstanding leadership have been an inspiration to his regiment and have directly contributed throughout the mixed and heavy fighting of the 1944 Italian campaign to successive defeats of the enemy.'

As with the smaller campaigns of the interwar period, awards for the post-1945 'retreat from empire' operations were awarded in relatively small numbers, the most for Korea (65) and Malaya (27), with appropriately smaller numbers for operations in Kenya, the Far East (Borneo and Brunei), Aden and Palestine. Interestingly, no fewer than 17 were awarded to Australian personnel for the Vietnam War; these are exceptionally rare. More recently, 17 went to naval officers in the Falklands campaign of 1982 and four to the Army, 10 to Army and RAF officers for the Iraq War of 1991, nearly 40 (including Bars) for recent operations in Afghanistan and about 20 for Iraq operations between 2003-10.

The DSO was rendered obsolete as a gallantry decoration as a result of the honours reforms of 1993 but was retained as an award for 'distinguished leadership' and opened to all ranks. The Conspicuous Gallantry Cross (qv) is taken to be its replacement as a reward for gallantry.

# THE INDIAN ORDER OF MERIT

The very first official campaign medals and gallantry awards were produced by the Honourable East India Company (HEIC). The Order of Merit (after 1902 known as the Indian Order of Merit) was instituted in 1837 to reward the gallantry of the HEIC's Indian soldiers; it was not awarded to the European soldiers of the HEIC or to British soldiers serving on campaign alongside HEIC forces.

The Order was established in three classes, 1st, 2nd and 3rd, with recipients technically having to be in possession of a lower grade before being promoted to the next – though there are known cases of direct appointments into the higher classes in cases of repeated gallantry in one period. The badge of the 3rd Class took the form of a star in silver and blue enamel, the 2nd Class in silver and blue enamel with a gold central wreath

*(Left) The Order of Merit, 1st Class, in gold, 1837-1911; a very rare award, with only 42 issued. It became obsolete in 1911 when the VC was opened to the Indian Army and the Order was reduced.*

*(Right) The Order of Merit, 1st type, 2nd Class, with gold wreath, 1837-1911.*

*(Left) The Order of Merit, 3rd Class, in silver, 1837-1911.*

*(Right) The typical reverse of an IOM badge; they are occasionally found engraved with the recipient's details.*

and the 1st Class entirely in gold. The award also conferred increased pay and pensions and, if the soldier was killed in action, the pension would go to his next of kin.

Always a rare medal, sparingly awarded and only conferred for actual gallantry in combat, it was very highly regarded and was often referred to as 'the Indian Victoria Cross' before 1911 when the VC itself was opened to Indian recipients. At that date, the Order was reduced to two classes, 1st and 2nd. The original central wording 'Reward of Valor' (sic) was altered to 'Reward of Gallantry' in 1939 and the Order was further reduced to one class in 1944. A civil version of the IOM was produced between 1902 and 1939, when it too was reduced to one class. But examples are excessively rare, with only 49 ever issued and actual examples seldom seen.

The reverse of all awards was plain, except for identifying the grade ('3rd Class Order of Merit' etc.), though they are sometimes found privately named to their recipient. The medal was worn from a wide dark blue ribbon with red edges, with an integral ribbon buckle.

*The short-lived and rare 4th type (single class 1944-47). A more ornate version, with decorated top pin brooch. Most were awarded for service in Burma.*

*Order of Merit, 2nd Class, 3rd type, 1939-45 with **Reward of Gallantry** centre.*

Between 1837 and 1911, when the Order was reduced, approximately 2,750 awards of the 3rd Class were made, with only 130 of the 2nd Class and only 42 of the 1st Class – which makes it one of the rarest of gallantry awards. Most of these were for the Indian Mutiny of 1857-59 and for larger campaigns like the Afghan War of 1878-80 and the rest for the smaller frontier wars of the late nineteenth century. An

*Order of Merit, 3rd Class, for the Indian Mutiny (Central India) in a group to a cavalryman of the Hyderabad Contingent.*

37

interesting example of the mass award of the decoration is the issue of approximately 1,100 IOMs, mainly of the 3rd Class, to the Indian soldiers who served in the defence of Lucknow in 1857. Their loyalty was vital to the success of the defence, at a time when they could easily have joined the mutinous Indian regiments besieging the Residency defences, and it was decided soon after the campaign that every one would receive the IOM. It is the largest mass award of a gallantry medal in British military history.

*The Afghan War IOM 3rd Class and campaign medals to Sepoy Hasan Khan, 24th Bengal Infantry – for gallantry in the Bazar Valley in 1879 in fighting off an attack on a signalling company.*

Undoubtedly the most famous recipient of the IOM in Victorian times was Kishanbir Nagarkoti of the 5th Gurkhas. He received the 3rd Class for gallantry in the fighting in the Mangiar Pass in Afghanistan in December 1878, was advanced to the 2nd Class for conspicuous gallantry in action at the battle of Charasia in October 1879 and then to the 1st Class for his gallantry in the fighting near Kabul on the 12th December 1879, when he went to the assistance of Lieutenant Fasken, 3rd Sikhs, who was wounded and lying under hostile fire. Three awards of the IOM – and all in one campaign – is some record, but Nagarkoti posed the authorities a considerable problem when as an officer (Subadar) he was again recommended for his outstanding gallantry in a rearguard action during the Hazara campaign of 1888. But, since he already held the 1st Class of the Order, there was no class of IOM left to give him and no other gallantry reward available to Indian soldiers. So the authorities hit upon the novel and (as it turned out) unique expedient of awarding Nagarkoti a gold Bar to his gold IOM, reflecting a truly outstanding record of gallantry in action. He became the only soldier who ever received what were in effect four awards of the IOM!

During World War I, 1914-18, only 953 awards of the 2nd Class were made and only 20 of the 1st Class (remembering that these were promotions from the 2nd Class). The largest numbers were conferred for service in Mesopotamia (approximately 415, of which 10 were to the 1$^{st}$ Class), France and Flanders (243, of which four were to the 1st Class) and Egypt (148), with correspondingly smaller numbers for the other theatres like Gallipoli, East Africa, and Persia. Compare these figures with well over 120,000 Military Medals and Bars awarded just between 1916-19.

*The IOM 2nd Class, with WWI medals. An award for service in Mesopotamia, where the largest numbers of Indian soldiers were deployed and where 400 IOMs were earned.*

Relatively small numbers were awarded during the interwar period (e.g. for Iraq 1919-20 and for small-scale operations) – only five awards of the 1st Class and 225 of the 2nd, mainly for service on the North West Frontier of India and especially for the various Waziristan campaigns before 1939.

For World War II, there were only two 1st Class awards and 332 of the 2nd Class. The post-1944 single-class is even rarer – only 30 were ever conferred. This gives a total of only 364 awards for the entire war, most being granted for Burma, Italy and North Africa. At only twice the number of Victoria Crosses for WWII, this is an astonishingly low number at a time when the Indian Army was expanded literally into millions, serving all over the world. These low award figures do not indicate any lack of gallantry on the part of Indian soldiers but rather the very demanding requirements that were set for this highly-rated award. Compare these IOM award figures with, say, the 10,400 Military Crosses or over 15,000 Military Medals for WWII.

Amongst the many actions which earned the IOM over the years, that by Havildar (later Subadar Major) Bhimbahadur Sen, 1-9th Gurkhas, for North Africa in 1943, stands as a good example of the level of gallantry required, as related in the original recommendation:

'During the attack at Point 166 (at Medjez el Bab) this NCO displayed most conspicuous and gallant leadership, determination and devotion to duty. On reaching the foremost part of the objective under heavy mortar and machine gun fire, Havildar Bhim Bahadur, who was in command of the forward platoon, found that the heaviest enemy resistance was coming from an uppermost system of trenches some distance further on. Collecting his platoon, he drew his kukri and placing himself at its head, led them straight at these trenches under close and intense fire. Reaching the first enemy post, he rushed it, personally killing all its occupants with his kukri.

He then led his men on to the remaining trenches which were quickly overcome by the fierceness and determination of his attack. With cool judgement and continued disregard for his personal safety, he then proceeded under heavy enemy defensive fire to reorganise securely the captured objective against the expected counter-attack. His determination, leadership and personal gallantry were an inspiring example to his men and were the main factors in enabling the objective to be so quickly and completely secured.'

The Indian Order of Merit, along with all other British-Indian decorations, became obsolete in 1947 when India was granted Independence.

*Sepoy Mihan Singh, 92nd Punjabis, earns the Order of Merit – crawling out alone into no-man's land to shoot down enemy soldiers preparing to attack his regiment's position.*

# THE DISTINGUISHED SERVICE CROSS

The award of a gallantry decoration specifically for junior commissioned officers and senior warrant officers of the Royal Navy can be traced to the institution of the Conspicuous Service Cross (CSC) in June 1901. The decoration was only conferred on eight occasions prior to the death of Edward VII in 1910, so that examples are very rare, especially to identifiable recipients (e.g. with other named medals). One such award was the unique Somaliland CSC conferred on to Lt. Commander A. G. Onslow, Royal Navy, for gallantry at Illig in 1904, where he made several gallant charges under point-blank fire through burning huts into concealed caves to attack tribesmen who were firing at the British assault force.

*The original Conspicuous Service Cross – an excessively rare award.*

With the onset of war in 1914, the award was revived by Order in Council of 14th October 1914, re-designated as the Distinguished Service Cross (DSC). It was to be conferred on officers and warrant officers below the rank of Lieutenant

Commander in the Royal Navy, Royal Naval Reserve, Royal Naval Air Service and (after 1916) the Royal Indian Marine. It was formally extended to the appropriate ranks of the Merchant and Fishing fleets in 1931 (though some had actually been awarded to these services in WWI), in 1940 to the Royal Air Force and in 1942 to army personnel serving afloat. The award was also conferred on Commonwealth personnel.

The original CSC took the form of a very plain silver cross, with rounded ends to its convex arms, the obverse bearing the cypher of Edward VII under a crown, within a roundel. It retained the same design after its re-designation in 1914, carrying the cypher of the appropriate reigning monarch in the centre. The reverse is hallmarked, but otherwise plain,

*Obverse and reverse of the DSC, George V type.*

though they are frequently found privately engraved with the recipient's details and after c. 1940 the Cross bore the year of the award engraved on the lower arm. As of January 1984, the decoration is officially named on the reverse to its recipient. Slightly concave slip-on Bars, bearing a central crown, were authorised in 1916 to reward further service and these too have the date of award on their reverse after 1940. The ribbon is dark blue with a central stripe of white, in equal proportions.

As usual, notifications of award are published in *The London Gazette*. For 1914-18 service, approx. 1,800 Crosses, 100 Bars and 10 second Bars were conferred, with some awards being made for post-war operations in Russia and only seven for operations during the interwar years (mainly for China and Palestine).

Given the global range of Royal Navy activities in both world wars and beyond, the DSC has understandably been awarded for a wide variety of actions – from convoy escort and minesweeping, to submarine actions, naval air service raids, ship-to-ship combats, landings and larger fleet operations.

*Obverse of the 1st type George VI DSC, with royal and imperial (Indian) cypher, 1937-47.*

Many WWI DSCs have fairly bland citations, as published in *The London Gazette*, often just giving the theatre of war, nature of operations and date, a fairly typical example being 'For

*The Bar to the DSC.*

*DSC with standard WWI medals.*

44

services in Minesweeping Operations between the 1st July and 31st December, 1918.' However, official recommendations and other sources can provide some outstanding examples of bravery in action.

One example is the award to James McDonald Dunbar of the Merchant Navy, whose DSC was announced in *The London Gazette* on 17th March 1919: 'In recognition of zeal and devotion to duty shown in carrying on the trade of the country during the War.' However, other sources make it clear that the

*DSC medal with Mercantile Marine awards awarded to J. M. Dunbar. Officers of the Merchant Navy and fishing fleets were given the DSC during the First World War, though not officially recognised as entitled until 1931.*

award was for 'gallantry on the occasion of the attack on [the S.S. *Caspian*] by an enemy submarine on the 20th May 1917.' S.S. *Caspian* was sailing from Chile to Italy with a cargo of nitrate when attacked by the German U-Boat U-34 in the early hours of 20th May 1917 off Cape Palos, Spain. What followed was 'a fight to the finish, which lasted for two hours', when the out-ranged gun of the *Caspian* tried to fight off the U-Boat. The ship was hit eight times and suffered severe damage, expending all 100 rounds of her ammunition without ever reaching the submarine. The Master and five crewmen were killed by gunfire and altogether 25 lives were lost, including some who died from exposure in open boats once the ship had been abandoned. Dunbar and two others were taken prisoner and the *Caspian* was finally sunk by a torpedo.

The Second World War saw a much larger award of the DSC, with about 4,500 conferred, with about 450 Bars, 44 second Bars and (remarkably) one with three Bars. The only person ever awarded the Distinguished Service Cross four times was Norman Eyre Morley, who served in the Royal Naval Reserve during both wars. He was awarded the DSC for the first time in 1919, winning the first Bar in 1944 and the other two in 1945. Unsurprisingly, he features in *The Guinness Book of Records* as the most decorated naval reserve officer.

*A fine WWII group with DSC and a range of campaign awards and with 'mentioned in dispatches' emblem.*

As an example of a wartime DSC award, we may consider that to Lieutenant F. Miller, Royal Navy, announced in *The London Gazette* on 22nd December 1942: 'For gallantry and distinguished service in the battles of Crete and Cape Matapan, while serving in HMS *Nubian*.' Born in 1900, Miller was perhaps rather older than the usual naval lieutenant and had served through World War I. On the outbreak of hostilities in 1939, he was aboard the destroyer *Nubian* and saw active service off Norway in April 1940, where she was 'bombed out' of the fjords near Trondheim. *Nubian* then served in the Mediterranean, supporting the *Warspite* in action with the Italian Fleet off Calabria in July 1940. It was, however, for *Nubian*'s part in the battle of Cape Matapan on 28th March 1941, that Miller won his DSC, when as Gunner he was responsible for firing the torpedoes that sank the Italian cruiser *Pola*. Next month, *Nubian* was engaged during a successful action with an Italian convoy off Sfax, and then assisted in operations during the withdrawal from Greece. On 26th May 1941, during the Crete operations, *Nubian* was badly damaged by enemy aircraft while escorting the *Formidable* for her attack on Scarpanto. Seven of her crew were killed and another 12 wounded. Flooding in the stern section of the ship was so extensive that her commander – on Miller's suggestion to 'keep the boys busy' – gave orders to fire all the torpedoes and jettison everything that would help lighten the ship. An attack was made on the crippled ship an hour later by five bombers, but she managed to dodge the bombs and reach harbour without further damage.

*A DSC with second award Bar, for minesweeping operations in World War II.*

For the Korean War, approximately 65 crosses were awarded, with 16 Bars. In the smaller post-war 'end of empire' campaigns, the Cross was granted only in very small numbers e.g. for the Yangtze, the Near East (Suez) and for Malaysia and surrounding areas. Even though approximately 28 were conferred for the Falklands campaign of 1982, fewer than 160 DSCs and Bars have been awarded since the end of the Second World War, so that modern examples are rarely seen.

*DSC with cypher of Elizabeth II. Note date of award carried on reverse.*

*The unique 1982 'Defence of South Georgia' DSC group awarded to Lieutenant K. P. Mills, Royal Marines; aged just 22, Mills led his small group of men in the defence of King Edward Point, against an overwhelming Argentine attack.*

With the reform of the honours system in 1993, the DSC was retained but made available to all ranks, the Distinguished Service Medal (qv) being rendered obsolete.

# THE MILITARY CROSS

Very early in World War I it was realised that the existing gallantry awards did not adequately cover the type of leadership and bravery being displayed in action, especially on the Western Front and by junior officers. Accordingly, in December 1914, a new army gallantry award was instituted – the Military Cross (MC) – essentially to reward senior NCOs and junior officers, below the 'Field Officer' rank of Major.

The medal was a simple, silver Greek cross, with the royal cypher in the centre (altered for successive monarchs) and imperial crowns at the ends of splayed arms; the reverse is flat and plain, though examples are often found privately engraved with the recipient's personal details. From 1938 to c.1960s, the year of award (which is not necessarily the year of the act for which it was awarded) was engraved on the reverse of the lower arm of the Cross or the reverse of a later award Bar. This practice was recently revived. The ribbon is white with a central purple stripe and is attached to the Cross by means of a very plain, flat suspender.

*The Military Cross, WWI era. The reverse is plain but is often found privately engraved with the recipient's details, date of action, date of award etc.*

From 1916, Bars, which were simply slipped onto the ribbon, could be awarded to reflect subsequent awards for acts of bravery. When ribbons alone

49

are worn, the possession of a Bar is indicated by a silver rosette (or rosettes) worn in the centre of the ribbon.

The MC could also be conferred on officers of the Royal Flying Corps, the RAF, the Royal Marines and Royal Navy for service in land operations, on members of the imperial forces at the appropriate rank (e.g. Canadians, Australians, Indians); it could also be conferred on foreign recipients (e.g. American, Belgian or French personnel) as allies of Great Britain – nearly 3000 of these being given for WWI. The decoration has been awarded for all theatres of war in which British and imperial forces found themselves on campaign since 1914 to date, including the North West Frontier of India, Palestine, Korea, Malaya, the Far East, the Falklands, Iraq, Afghanistan etc.

*An example of the Military Cross with second award Bar.*

The fact of an award was notified in *The London Gazette* or similar official journals (like *The Gazette of India*) which sometimes published the citation – usually some time after the initial announcement; recommendations are also found in The National Archives, but not all survive or are publicly available. Regimental and campaign histories, war diaries and contemporary newspapers may also explain the background to the award.

During World War I, approximately 37,000 single MCs were awarded, with approximately 3,000 first Bars, 169 second Bars and only four third Bars.

An example of a World War I award, for gallantry near Fontaine during the battle of Cambrai in 1917, is that to the 19-year-old Lieutenant Edward A. Crane of 75 Field Company, Royal

*The MC and 1914 medal group to Lieutenant H. R. Glen – a very early award to the Army Service Corps for service in 1914.*

*The Military Cross, WWI period, with two additional Bars – approx. 169 awarded.*

Engineers. The citation, following the usual statement in such awards that it was 'for conspicuous gallantry and devotion to duty', went on to relate that 'during an attack, under continuous and intense shell fire, he repaired and cleared a light railway track, bringing back the trucks on the line with an enemy tractor under its own power. This line proved invaluable in bringing back the wounded to the advanced dressing station. He supervised the maintenance of this line until severely wounded.'

*The fine Western Front Military Cross group to Lt. (later Colonel) E. A. Crane, RE – at the start of a long and distinguished career.*

In the interwar years, the MC was of course awarded for smaller colonial operations, from the Iraq Rebellion of 1919-20, to the many Indian frontier campaigns (to the Indian Army as well as British units) and for Palestine, among others. Approximately 350 MCs were gazetted between 1920-1939, with 31 Bars. In World War II, approximately 10,400 MCs were conferred, with 482 first Bars and 24 second Bars.

Major H. R. Steele of the 5th Mahratta Light Infantry, Indian Army, received his initial MC for gallantry in the famous action at Sangshak in Burma in May 1944, where he ambushed an enemy patrol and later led an attack against a Japanese position 'with great speed and dash' and then held the

*The Military Cross, with 1st type George VI cypher of 1937-47. It was replaced after Indian independence with GviR.*

*The MC and Bar group to Major H. R. Steele, 5th Mahratta Light Infantry.*

position against 'fierce enemy attacks till ordered to withdraw'. The Bar was awarded for his outstanding gallantry in action in November 1944, when he led two consecutive attacks on a well-defended hill position, under machine gun fire, and then withdrew to re-organise his shaken men. Fighting off several counter attacks, even though the enemy been reinforced and surrounded his position, he held the enemy back until he

*A campaign group with MC awarded for operations following the invasion of Iraq in 2003. 85 MCs were awarded for this theatre.*

could organise an effective withdrawal and also succeeded in removing all his wounded. Throughout the action, his men were under heavy rifle, mortar and machine-gun fire at close range.

As examples of numbers for other campaigns, 182 single MCs were awarded for Korea (1951-54), 139 for Malaya, 16 for the Falklands War in 1982, approximately 85 for recent campaigns in Iraq and nearly 200 for recent operations in Afghanistan. They are understandably scarce for some of the smaller colonial campaigns and more recent operations.

Following the honours reforms of 1993, when actual *medals* for gallantry (e.g. the Military Medal) were abolished, the MC was opened to all ranks and it remains to this day one of the principal rewards for gallantry in action. Such awards have been made for recent operations in the Balkans, Iraq and Afghanistan and they are of course now awarded to female personnel.

*The 2011 Afghanistan MC group awarded to Bugle Major J. A. Davies, The Rifles, who instinctively took command of his Company after a massive improvised explosive device caused severe injuries; leading by personal example, Davies brought the Company to safety and was recommended for the CGC.*

# THE DISTINGUISHED FLYING CROSS

The formation of the Royal Air Force in 1918, amalgamating the Royal Flying Corps and the Royal Naval Air Service, led to the creation of new awards for air combat. The Distinguished Flying Cross (DFC) was introduced as a reward for Warrant Officers and commissioned officers of the RAF and the Distinguished Flying Medal (qv) for NCOs and Other Ranks.

The Air Force Cross and Air Force Medal (qv) were their non-combatant equivalents.

The decoration was instituted, along with the other new aerial forces' awards, by Royal Warrant and *London Gazette* of 3rd June 1918. It was to be conferred for 'an act or acts of valour, courage or devotion to duty performed whilst on active operations against the enemy'. Bars for subsequent awards were authorised in the original warrant; these take the form of the silver slip-on type, with the RAF eagle device in the centre.

*The Distinguished Flying Cross, showing the ornate obverse.*

*The Bar to the DFC*

The medal was designed by the prolific sculptor and designer Edward Carter Preston and is rather elaborate. It comprises an ornate cross *flory*, with bombs at the end of three arms and a rose on the upper one; superimposed on this is a second cross, formed of propellers, in the centre of which is a winged roundel of laurel bearing a rose, with RAF. The reverse is plain except for a central roundel containing the reigning monarch's monogram and 1918, the date of institution. The decoration was issued unnamed but is often seen with the recipient's details privately engraved to the reverse; after 1939, the year of award was engraved on the reverse lower arm.

*The obverse and reverse of the standard Distinguished Flying Cross, with post 1919 diagonal striped ribbon.*

The suspension takes the form of a shaped and decorated bar carrying a ribbon of violet and white stripes. As originally designed, the stripes were horizontal but in June 1919 they were altered to left-right diagonals.

Surprisingly, given the late appearance of the DFC, approx. 1,050 DFCs and 73 Bars were awarded for the latter stages of WWI and immediate post-war operations. An early award of the DFC, to Lieutenant G. F. M. Apps, of 66 (Sopwith Camel) Squadron, gives a flavour of the type of skill and gallantry which could be rewarded by the new decoration. Gazetted on 21st September 1918, its published citation simply awarded the DFC to Apps as 'A bold and skilful airman who in recent operations has destroyed six enemy aeroplanes, accounting for two in one flight. He displays marked determination and devotion to duty.'

*War in the air: one of the novelties of WWI which led to the creation of a new series of air awards in 1918.*

*A WWI award of the DFC, with the original horizontal striped ribbon which was quickly altered to the diagonal type. With two WWI medals.*

As is commonly the case, this brief reference masks an extraordinary career of active air combat over only six months, during which, in over 100 sorties above the Italian front, he brought down at least ten enemy aircraft. He carried out his first offensive patrols in January 1918 and was to remain actively employed until being wounded on 17th July. Apps gained his first confirmed victory north of Valstagna on 11th March; on 28th March, in a combat over Oderzo, he destroyed an Albatross D. III and on 4th May, while patrolling over Vidor, Apps shot down an enemy fighter over the River Piave. He was then attacked head on by a D. III, this being repeated on four occasions, on the last of which the enemy plane went down out of control and crashed at Moriago. In a combat on 20th May, Apps chased down a D.V. which had been shot up by his Squadron Leader and a few days later, on the 24th, he claimed another confirmed D. III, following a fifteen minute combat above Mount Coppolo. On 21st June, during an offensive patrol over Motta, Apps brought down a D.III, which crashed near Sala di La and having then destroyed another Albatross D. III over Chromenti on 28th June, he shot down another one in combat south of Godega on 13th July. Finally, on 16th July, he shared in the destruction of an L.V.G. south-west of Posimone. The following day he was seriously wounded in the right leg by anti-aircraft fire, effectively ending his active service. He returned to the UK and joined 50 Squadron as a Flight Commander on home service duties.

In the interwar years, 140 DFCs with 24 Bars were conferred, the majority for service on the North West Frontier of India. The DFC is, strange as it seems, the commonest gallantry award for service on the North West Frontier between the wars.

The World War II award figures are unsurprisingly much higher, reflecting the more extensive use of aerial forces (mass bombing and air combat) during the period. Over 20,000 DFCs were awarded for WWII, with approximately 1,600 Bars. They were generally awarded in two forms – as a 'periodic' award for distinguished service over a long period (e.g. participating in a large number of successful raids) or as an 'immediate' award for a specific act or acts of gallantry.

Just one example (of many) of the type of DFC awarded for

protracted and dedicated service, rather than for a specific act of gallantry, is that awarded to a Whitley bomber pilot, Group Captain L. W. Howard, of 77 Squadron, Royal Air Force. The decoration was announced in *The London Gazette* of 23rd May 1941 in the usual terse fashion:

> 'This officer has commanded an operational flight since July 1940. During this period he has taken part in numerous attacks on important targets in Germany, and also on the enemy occupied port of Bordeaux. He has at all times displayed a fine spirit in the execution of these flights, and has set and maintained a high standard of operational efficiency throughout his command.'

In earning his DFC, Howard had flown in 25 operational sorties with the Squadron, including several raids on Kassel Aircraft Factory (19th, 21st and 23rd August 1940), Bottrop, Wismar, Frankfurt, Bremen (x3), Mannheim, Berlin (x3), Stettin, Wesserling, Magdeburg, Cologne, Hanover (x2), Bordeaux, Merignac Airfield, Wilhelmshaven and Gelsenkirchen. Twenty of these raids were carried out in 1940 and no doubt any one could tell a story in itself; many RAF aircrew served in more operations than this and far from all of them received any form of decoration.

A gallantry DFC was that conferred on Squadron Leader R. C. Chopping, Royal Air Force Volunteer Reserve, who spent the first part of the war flying Bombays and Hudsons over Africa with Transport Command, before transferring to Bomber Command in September 1943. An exceptional Lancaster pilot with 514 Squadron, he flew in 28 operational sorties with the Squadron, with his Air Gunners claiming 4 enemy night fighters damaged. Chopping was awarded the DFC (*London Gazette* 21st July 1944) for gallant conduct during an abortive raid to Dortmund on 22nd  May 1944. The detailed recommendation stated:

> 'Squadron Leader R. C. Chopping has successfully completed twenty-four bombing sorties as the Pilot and Captain of Lancaster aircraft. He is a most experienced Captain, keen and enthusiastic,

*The DFC group to Squadron Leader Chopping.*

and the photographs he has obtained bear out the excellence of his work. On the night of 24th February, when returning from an attack on Schweinfurt he was attacked by an enemy fighter, which he outmanoeuvred and which his gunners claim to have damaged. The following night he had three combats with night fighters during a raid on Augsberg. Each attack was broken and two of the enemy fighters were damaged by the Air Gunners.

At Stuttgart, on the 2nd March, 1944, Squadron Leader Chopping's aircraft received a direct hit and he had to return on three engines, while on the 19th, May, 1944, his aircraft was again badly damaged by anti-aircraft fire when crossing the French coast. On this occasion the port wing was badly holed and the Wireless Operator was knocked unconscious, but despite this Squadron Leader Chopping continued to the target at Le Mans, and bombed it successfully.

On the night of 22nd May shortly after setting course for Dortmund, this Officer encountered

very severe icing conditions, in cloud, at a height of 10,000 feet. Violent vibration occurred and the aircraft, losing speed, began to lose height at an alarming rate, quite out of control. Squadron Leader Chopping ordered his crew to abandon the aircraft, which they reluctantly did; but, because his bomb load included a 8,000 lb. bomb, and he feared the damage this might do if it fell in this country, he remained in the aircraft hoping to regain control. The aircraft broke cloud at 2,500 feet and not until then did he manage to regain control. He flew out over the North sea to jettison his bombs and made an emergency landing at Woodbridge.

Since that time he has completed seven more successful bombing operations, has been involved in a further fighter attack, and claims one more enemy fighter damaged.'

Sadly, Squadron Leader Chopping was killed with all his crew in action over Brest on 25th/26th August 1944.

As is usual with British gallantry awards, post-war numbers are much lower, reflecting the smaller scale of air operations

*The Second World War fighter ace's DFC group awarded to Wing Commander F. M. 'Hiram' Smith, Royal Air Force, a gallant Canadian pilot whose name remains indelibly linked to the Battle of Britain.*

during post-war and imperial campaigns, with nearly 90 for Korea, over 100 for Malaya (1948-60) and smaller numbers for the Far East, Aden and South Arabia. Nine (amongst all services) were awarded for the Falklands campaign in 1982, nine and three Bars for Iraq 2003-10 and 25 DFCs and one Bar have so far been awarded for recent operations in Afghanistan.

In fact, since the start of the present queen's reign, a total of 385 Crosses (including 26 Bars) has been gazetted, of which about half were conferred on RAF personnel, with more than 50 presented to members of the British army and navy and around 140 Commonwealth awards, mainly to Australians for Vietnam. Only two women have received the DFC, the first being gazetted in 2008 for Iraq, to Flight Lieutenant Michelle Goodman. She was captain of a Merlin Incident Reaction Team, when, on 1st June 2007, she flew into Basra at night using night vision and under heavy fire to evacuate a seriously wounded soldier of the 4th Rifles (who had been given just minutes to live following a mortar attack). Her DFC was gazetted on 7th March 2008.

Following the honours reforms of 1993, the DFC became available to all ranks (as has the AFC) and the DFM and AFM ceased to be awarded.

# THE AIR FORCE CROSS

The formation of the Royal Air Force in April 1918, combining the Royal Naval Air Service and the Royal Flying Corps, provided the opportunity to create a new series of awards specifically for aerial services. One result was the institution of the Distinguished Flying Cross and Distinguished Flying Medal (qv) as awards for gallantry in air combat. But it was also decided to create two equivalent awards – the Air Force Cross and the Air Force Medal – to reward distinguished services in the air which were not in combat or 'in the face of the enemy'.

The Air Force Cross (AFC) was an Officers' and Warrant Officers' award instituted by Royal Warrant and *London Gazette* of 3rd June 1918, as with the other new air force decorations. The award, designed by Edward Carter Preston, took the form of an elaborate silver cross, below a crown, the arms in the form of thunderbolts joined by feathered wings. This design has superimposed on it another cross formed of propeller blades, the ends bearing the letters G – R – V – I and the lower arm ending with a bomb. A central roundel depicts Hermes, mounted on a flying hawk, proffering a wreath. The reverse is flat and plain, except for a central roundel carrying the reigning monarch's cypher

*The ornate obverse of the Air Force Cross.*

and 1918 as date of institution. It is sometimes seen with the recipient's details privately engraved on the reverse, though since January 1984 they have been officially named.

*The AFC, obverse and reverse. With original horizontally striped ribbon.*

*An example of the very rare AFC with second award Bar, in this case with WWII campaign medals for Burma and Italy.*

The medal is suspended from an ornamented bar. The ribbon originally comprised thin horizontal stripes of red and white but this was altered in July 1919 to left-right diagonal stripes of those colours. Bars, of standard slip-on type, with the RAF eagle motif to the centre, were authorised for further services; awards with Bars are rare and only about 20 AFCs have been awarded with two Bars.

The AFC was the non-combatant equivalent of the DFC (qv) and was granted 'for exceptional valour, courage or devotion to duty whilst flying, though not in active operations against the enemy'. Examples of such service are test flights over a long period, air-sea rescue, transport duties, training etc.; gallantry on a specific occasion or meritorious service over a longer period could lead to the award of the decoration. The AFC was awarded to British and Commonwealth personnel and honorary awards can be made to non-Commonwealth recipients.

Notifications of award are published, as usual, in *The London Gazette*, but citations did not often appear in its pages and it can be difficult to establish the exact circumstances of award, especially for those which reward a long period of training, experimental or rescue work.

*An example of a WWI Air Force Cross, with campaign medals.*

One such example is that to Captain W. J. J. Badenhorst, South African Air Force. Having seen service as a Spitfire Pilot during the Second War, he served as a Flight Commander with 2 (Cheetah) Squadron SAAF during the Korean War, 1950-53 and was awarded the American Distinguished Flying Cross and the US Air Medal with 3 Oak Leaf Clusters. However, he had before this time earned the Air Force Cross, gazetted in *The London Gazette* of 4th June 1946.

The Recommendation states:

> 'This Officer has completed an Operational Tour and has, in addition, carried out 1470 hours as a Flying Instructor, 110 of which have been done during the last six months. He has completed over 2,200 hours Service Flying. He is a most efficient and conscientious Flight Commander. His flying and instruction is of a high order and his assessment of pupils' ability very sound.'

The AFC has always been a scarce award, with fewer than 5,000 conferred to date. Only about 850 were given between the decoration's creation in 1918 and the outbreak of World War II, and about 2,000 were conferred for 1939-45. As with other Crosses for gallantry, the AFC was opened to all ranks for operational gallantry (but no longer for long and meritorious service) following the reforms of 1993.

*A WWII Air Force Cross in a group with the Air Efficiency Award (right).*

# THE DISTINGUISHED CONDUCT MEDAL

The Distinguished Conduct Medal was the first official reward for gallantry created within the British system of honours. It was one of three decorations born out of the Russian War of 1854-56 and more particularly for the Crimean War. The land campaign in the Crimea was the first to be widely reported in the British press, with detailed accounts appearing in national and local newspapers. They brought home to the reading public the reality of the conditions of warfare, the mismanagement of the army and the gallantry of the forces engaged. A number of what came to be known as 'war correspondents' were employed by various newspapers, the most famous being W. H. Russell (later Lord Russell) of *The Times*. This in-depth press coverage brought home to the British public the reality of the situation in the Crimea and the reaction to it finally spurred the government into creating a national system of gallantry awards.

As a result, three decorations were instituted – the Distinguished Conduct Medal (DCM) for the Other Ranks of the Army, the Conspicuous Gallantry Medal (CGM) for the Ratings and Other Ranks of the Royal Navy and Royal Marines and the Victoria Cross (VC).

*A Crimean War DCM to a Sgt. in the 33rd Regt. for gallantry at Inkermann and with a French* **Medaille Militaire** *awarded for gallantry 'before Sebastopol'.*

The Distinguished Conduct Medal was authorised by Royal Warrant of 4th December 1854 and first presented in 1855, the award being made retrospective to the start of the war in February 1854. It was to be awarded for 'distinguished, gallant and good conduct in the field', and could be conferred on all ranks in the Army below commissioned officer; it came to be the second highest award for gallantry in action following the slightly later institution of the Victoria Cross (1856). It was awarded with a gratuity, which varied in amount depending on rank, and was given on the recipient's discharge from the Army. The medal was always much coveted and very highly regarded.

*The standard obverse of the DCM, 1854-1902, with the Pistrucci 'trophy of arms' design.*

The circular silver medal was of standard dimensions (36 mm diameter) and bore on its obverse a fine 'trophy of arms' design by Benedetto Pistrucci of the Royal Mint; this was already in use on the Army Long Service and Good Conduct Medal and was only altered in 1902 when the profile and usual titles of the reigning monarch were adopted in its place. The reverse was rather plain, simply bearing the words FOR DISTINGUISHED CONDUCT IN THE FIELD. The medal was attached to a swivelling scroll type suspension, though later in the twentieth century fixed suspensions were used. The ribbon was crimson with a central dark blue stripe.

*The standard obverse of the DCM from 1854-1993.*

The DCM was extended to other armed services, like colonial and associated forces, but not to Indian soldiers who were deemed to have their own system of awards, with the Indian Order of Merit (1837) and Indian Distinguished Service Medal (1907). Later, a few awards were made on occasion to Royal Navy, Royal Naval Division, Royal Marines and RAF recipients serving in association with land operations, but in general these forces were rewarded with their own service-appropriate decorations. The DCM was also conferred on foreign recipients for service with British forces in both world wars, but such awards were not usually named and often not gazetted.

Bars to the DCM, to recognise additional acts of gallantry, were authorised in 1881 and up until September 1916 bore the date or dates of the action for which the award was made (e.g. SEPTEMBER 1st 1880 or NOVEMBER 21st – 24th 1899) and were affixed to the medal suspension like campaign medal clasps. After that, the Bars took the from of the standard laurelled slip-on type, presumably because they were simpler to produce and issue at a time of increasing numbers of awards. Prior to 1901, the date of the action was sometimes engraved on the rim of the medal, along with the usual naming details, but this was not always done. As of 1917 awards were to be made only to the 'fighting

*The George V DCM with second award Bar of the usual slide-on laurelled type.*

services' and from 1920, to be made for gallantry 'in action', or 'in the face of the enemy' and not, as had been done occasionally, to reward service behind the lines.

The official recommendations for the DCM are held in The National Archives in Kew but they are fragmentary (with many missing for the pre-1914 period) and do not often give any detail. As usual with British decorations, awards were announced in *The London Gazette* and similar official publications (like *The Edinburgh Gazette*) but in the years before World War One, there is generally little in the way of a citation, the usual wording being 'for recent operations in South Africa' or the like. Occasionally, some brief indication of the reason for the award is actually given in the *Gazette*, as with Sapper F. Trask of 37 Company, Royal Engineers, who was awarded the DCM for 'coolness and gallant behaviour when constructing a sandbag wall across the railway bridge at Langerwachte Spruit under heavy fire'. This was during the operations for the relief of Ladysmith in February 1900 and allowed the attacking troops to take some sort of shelter as they rushed over the bridge towards Boer lines. As with other British gallantry awards, extra detail can often be found in regimental or unit histories or in newspaper accounts and obituaries.

*The Victorian DCM with first type obverse, as awarded for the Boer War of 1899-1902, with standard Queen's and King's campaign medals.*

*Boer War period DCM with the newly-adopted (1902) obverse showing the monarch's profile and titles.*

From 1894 onwards, various distinctive (and now rare) colonial types were authorised for Canada and Natal, with the name of the dominion or colony added to the reverse; planned versions for New South Wales and New Zealand are not known to have been produced. Distinctive versions were also awarded for the West African Frontier Force in 1905 and King's African Rifles from 1906, with those regimental designations included on the reverse. The last two had a variant ribbon, which was blue with a narrow central light green stripe, flanked on either side by a narrow stripe of maroon.

*An example of the rare colonial reverse, in this case for the colony of Natal. Very few of these types were ever issued.*

*(left) The King's African Rifles version of the DCM, reverse, with distinctive ribbon.*

*(Right) The West African Frontier Force DCM, reverse.*

Approximately 3,500 medals and 13 second award Bars were awarded prior to 1914 – not a large number considering the range and number of imperial campaigns being waged around the world during that period. For the war in the Crimea – the first occasion for the award of the medal – approximately 775 were conferred, with understandably smaller numbers being granted for colonial campaigns – e.g. 22 for New Zealand 1862-66, 33 for the Ashantee War of 1873-74, 16 for the South African (and Zulu) campaigns of 1877-79, 61 for the Afghan War of 1878-80, the rather large number of 21 for the brief and disastrous Boer War of 1880-81, 134 for various actions in Egypt and the Sudan between 1882 and 1889 and 87 for the Sudan campaign of 1898-99. The long-running Boer or South African War of 1899-1902 saw the award of approx. 2,050 DCMs, about one third of which bore the new obverse with the effigy and titles of King Edward VII. It is interesting to note that fewer than two dozen DCMs are known to have been awarded for the severe campaigning during the Indian Mutiny of 1857-59, compared to 182 VCs which were conferred for the same campaign!

*A Victorian DCM – an award for Abu Klea in the Sudan in January 1885.*

Not surprisingly many more DCMs and Bars were awarded for the two world wars. For World War One, just over 24,500 medals were awarded, with approximately 470 first Bars and nine second Bars. Some awards of the DCM for 1914-18 reflect gallantry and good service over a period of time; that to Company Sgt. Major D. F. MacIntyre of the Argyll and Sutherland Highlanders stands as an example: 'For conspicuous gallantry and devotion to duty. He has performed consistent good work throughout and has at all times set a splendid example of courage and determination.' (*London Gazette* 12th March 1917)

However, most First World War DCMs were awarded for specific actions or acts of gallantry – all of them

*The obverse and reverse of the DCM as awarded for 1914-18.*

distinctive in their own way. That for Sgt. J Walker of the 7th Argyll and Sutherland Highlanders must serve as just one example. The award was gazetted on 18th July 1917 and the details published slightly later (as was usually the case):

'For conspicuous gallantry and devotion to duty. When all the officers had become casualties, he took charge of the remains of the company and succeeded in capturing and holding a village in spite of heavy artillery and machine gun fire.'

As usual with published citations, this brief account is only part of the story. Walker's company (his battalion serving as part of the 51st Highland Division) was attacking German positions at and around the defended chemical works and château in the village of Rouex during the battle of Arras in April 1917. With all his officers dead or out of action, Walker took control of the situation and actually led the attack which seized the whole village and then held it against German counter attacks – a remarkable achievement understandably rewarded with the DCM.

In the interwar years, with fewer occasions for the award of high-level decorations being offered, the DCM was rarely conferred – only about 45 for a range of theatres prior to 1939, and principally for the North West Frontier of India and Palestine. World War II led to the award of approximately 1,900 medals and 19 first Bars. Any study of the citations for the DCM for World War Two makes it immediately apparent that the standard required to win the medal was extremely high.

One example is the DCM awarded per *London Gazette* of 19th October 1944 to Sgt. Roland Clark, 1st Oxford and Bucks Light Infantry.'

'On 16th July 44 near Cahier 9062, Sgt. Clark took part in his Coy in Operation "Villa" in an artificially illuminated night attack on a small copse full of dense undergrowth. When just short of the objective a German MG 42 opened on the Coy and pinned it to the ground. Sgt. Clark, without hesitation, went forward alone and without orders over a distance of fifty yards and disappeared into the wood which was the Coy's objective. He re-emerged a few moments later carrying the German MG 42 on his shoulder and driving a German prisoner before him. Sgt. Clark had killed the remaining members of the team. By this remarkable action his Company was able to reach its objective. Thereafter in spite of a GSW in the leg which he persisted in describing as a "twisted knee" Sgt. Clark showed a coolness and courage beyond all praise during some three hours of hand to hand fighting. The intensity of the fighting was such that one Officer, eight effective NCOs and eighteen privates were killed and eighteen wounded in his Company.'

*The George VI DCM in a group; an award for North West Europe 1944-45.*

Clark was originally recommended for the Victoria Cross, but it was downgraded to a DCM, his being one of only 31 such downgrades from an original VC as recommended to a DCM, but similar downgrades between other awards (e.g. from DCM to MM and from MM to MID) are seen.

Post-war campaigns like the Korean War and the 'retreat from empire' operations, resulted in the award of only small numbers of DCMs – 24 for Korea, 49 for operations in Malaya 1948-60 (under both George VI and Elizabeth II), seven for the Arabian Peninsula 1959-75 and four for Borneo in the 1960s. No fewer than 75 were awarded to Australian forces for service in Vietnam prior to 1972. All are to be regarded as very rare and examples seldom seen.

As with other medals for gallantry, the venerable DCM was rendered obsolete as a result of the honours reforms of 1993; because of its history and status it was perhaps the most regretted loss of that reorganisation. The last ones awarded were nine for service in Northern Ireland after 1969, eight for the South Atlantic (Falklands) War of 1982 and eight for the Gulf War of 1991; these were, apart from a few retrospective or late awards, the last DCMs to be issued.

*An infantry attack during the Boer War; over 2,000 DCMs were awarded for the campaign.*

# THE CONSPICUOUS
# GALLANTRY MEDAL

The Conspicuous Gallantry Medal (CGM) was one of the three new gallantry awards introduced during the Russian War of 1854-56, the others being the Distinguished Conduct Medal and the Victoria Cross (qv).

The medal was introduced on 13th September 1855 and was intended to be the Royal Navy and Royal Marines' equivalent of the Distinguished Conduct Medal and, like the DCM, not available to officers.

The CGM has a curious early history. Despite the important contribution of the RN and RM to the campaigns associated with the war – in the Baltic, in the Black Sea and Sea of Azoff and ashore in the Crimea – only 11 awards were made (two going to one recipient, A.B. David Barry) and, since so few were required, the authorities exhibited an extraordinary degree of parsimony in simply taking examples of the existing Meritorious Service Medal (1845), erasing the words MERITORIOUS SERVICE on the reverse and simply engraving CONSPICUOUS GALLANTRY in their place.

Thereafter, the award seems to have lapsed, with no further medals being conferred (e.g. for campaigns in China 1856-60) until the Ashantee (Ashanti) war of 1873-74 in West Africa. The scale of the fighting there and the early and continued involvement of naval brigades led to the re-institution of the medal in July 1874. This time, it was properly manufactured and its suspension altered to the straight-bar type, though some Victorian awards after 1874 are found with scroll suspenders, as seen on the original adapted MSM versions of 1855. The earlier awards were not always gazetted, though recorded on the recipient's service record, but after 1901 details appear, as usual, in *The London Gazette*.

The ribbon was dark blue with a central white stripe until 1921, when it was altered to white with narrow dark blue edges; this

*The re-instituted CGM of 1874, obverse and reverse. With scroll suspension.*

was done to avoid confusion with the ribbon of the Distinguished Service Cross (qv). The medals are named around the rim in a variety of engraved styles and/or impressed upright capitals after 1882 reflecting the medal naming style of the time; some carry the year of the action on the rim and some show the name of the recipient's ship. The award was extended in April 1940 to RAF personnel serving on naval operations, to army personnel serving aboard defensively-armed merchant vessels in July 1942, to the Merchant Navy in September 1942 and to Dominion personnel in December 1943.

*The standard reverse of the CGM, 1874-1993. With straight bar suspension.*

The medal has always been very rare, those for the reign of Edward VII excessively so, with only two known. Prior to 1914, just over 50 were awarded (e.g. 12 for various actions in Egypt and the Sudan, 1882-85). During World War I, there were just over 100 awards and for 1939-45, only 72.

*The CGM with the very rare Edward VII obverse.*

Early awards of the CGM – in common with a number of Victorian gallantry awards – carried fairly brief citations in *The London Gazette*. One of the first of the re-instituted awards, one of only 22 CGMs for Ashantee 1873-74, was that to William Holloway, Quarter Master, of HMS *Rattlesnake*, conferred for 'the utmost coolness and intrepidity. Holloway was wounded on the occasion of the attack on our boats at Chamah in the River Prah [on 14th August 1873].'

A later Victorian example – its initial citation being typical of the brief details often given in the original *Gazette* – is one of the eight CGMs awarded for service in China in 1900. Able Seaman William Parsonage of HMS *Aurora* was gazetted for the medal simply 'in connection with recent operations in China', while his service record notes: 'Awarded the Conspicuous Gallantry Medal for services with the Naval Brigade in China 1900.' Announced in the *London Gazette* on 14th May 1901, the medal was personally presented by the King on 8th March 1902.

*Victorian CGM with medal for the Ashantee War and clasp* **Coomassie**.

However, as is often the case, more detail on the circumstances of the action can be gleaned from other accounts. Parsons was mentioned in the report of Vice Admiral Seymour, Naval Commander-in-Chief on the China Station, referring to operations at Tientsin between 10th and 26th June 1900: 'I desire to bring specially to Their Lordships' favourable notice the conduct of ... William Parsonage, A.B., of HMS *Aurora*, [who] ... assisted to carry Lieutenant G. B. Powell, wounded, to the rear, over open ground swept by rifle fire, and was wounded in so doing.' This was actually during the action of 19th June at Langfang, when 'two Chinese field guns were placed near the railway embankment opposite the British Concession [at Tientsin] and opened fire. Commander Beatty, with three companies of seamen, crossed the river and manoeuvred to within 200 or 300 yards in the hope of capturing them in a rush .... While our men were waiting for the Russians to come up, a large force of Chinese appeared to the right behind a mud wall and poured in a heavy fire, wounding Commander Beatty, Lieutenants Powell (*Aurora*) and Stirling (*Barfleur*), Mr. Donaldson, midshipman (*Barfleur*) ... and 11 men. The force then retired.'

It seems appropriate in choosing a WWI example to select the awards to Arthur Robert Blore. He was awarded the CGM and the only Bar to the CGM ever granted – which was of the standard laurelled slip-on type. As a Leading Seaman of the Royal Naval Volunteer Reserve, serving in the Anson Battalion of the Royal Naval Division, he was awarded the initial CGM for the Cape Helles landings on Gallipoli on 4th June 1915:

> 'The [Anson] battalion having occupied a portion of the enemy's fire trench on the 4th June, was engaged in digging communication trenches to a position in rear of it, on which they were consolidating the line. The officer being shot, Seaman Blore took charge of a party of 22, who advanced to cover the retirement. He shot two of the crew of a Turkish machine-gun enfilading the trench, and kept up a steady fire checking the enemy who were re-occupying it. He exhibited great bravery and power of leadership on a difficult occasion.' (*London Gazette*, 19th September 1915)

The Bar was conferred for service in France in September 1918, by which time Blore was Acting Chief Petty Officer:

> 'When all company officers had become casualties, and the company was held up by heavy machine-gun fire, this petty officer took command of the company. He reorganised and led the men forward by rushes to the enemy position. When about 100 yards from the position enemy fire became very heavy, and many casualties were caused to his command. Finding this, he went forward alone, and, single-handed, rushed the crew of a heavy machine gun, shooting the gunners. The enemy position was then turned, and thereby captured. By his initiative and personal courage a strong position was taken and many casualties avoided. Twenty-seven enemy machine guns, all of which were captured, were afterwards counted covering the ground over which this company advanced.' (*London Gazette*, 29th October 1918)

Blore went on to win the Military Medal – a remarkable series of awards. His medal group is held by the National Maritime Museum in Greenwich.

Petty Officer R. H. G. McKinlay earned his CGM in World War II for outstanding gallantry on D-Day, 6th June 1944 – one of only two awarded for the landings. It was gazetted on 29th August 1944: 'For gallantry, skill, determination and undaunted devotion to duty during the initial landings of Allied Forces on the coast of Normandy.'

*A CGM of WWII with the altered post-1921 ribbon.*

The official recommendation offers more detail:

> 'P.O. McKinlay landed between noon and 1400 hours on 6th June. Finding himself at some distance from his prearranged destination, he made his way along the beach and took charge of a party of Naval ratings and Army ranks who were bound for the same point. Single-handed, he silenced two enemy strong points on the way with hand grenades. Later, on an open stretch of sand which was under fire from enemy snipers, disregarding his own safety, he went to the rescue of a wounded man and brought him safely to cover.'

In more recent times, the CGM has remained an elusive award – one was conferred posthumously for the Falklands campaign in 1982 and one for Iraq in 1991. Only in the 1970s was eligibility for a number of British awards, including the CGM, extended to allow posthumous awards to be made; it is interesting to note that up until this time, only the Victoria Cross and a 'mention in dispatches' could be awarded posthumously.

In 1993, the Conspicuous Gallantry Medal was abolished, in common with other 'medals' for gallantry, its place effectively taken by the Conspicuous Gallantry Cross (qv).

# THE CONSPICUOUS
# GALLANTRY MEDAL (FLYING)

*A CGM (Flying) in WWII group with Air Crew Europe Star as awarded to Bomber Command.*

The original Conspicuous Gallantry Medal (qv) was introduced as an award for the Other Ranks of the Royal Navy and Royal Marines in 1855, during the Crimean War, as a counterpart to the Army's DCM (qv). Having lapsed, it was re-instituted in 1874 for the Ashantee War in West Africa and was always a rare award, infrequently conferred.

The CGM was extended to the NCOs and Other Ranks of the Royal Air Force as late as November 1942, as a higher-level award than the Distinguished Flying Medal, and in this form is known as the 'Conspicuous Gallantry Medal (Flying)'. It was exactly the same in design as the naval/marines' CGM, except that the ribbon was altered to feature a wide sky blue central stripe (rather than white), with dark blue edges.

*(Above) The reverse of the CGM (Flying) which it shares with the standard CGM.*

*(Left) The CGM (Flying), obverse; the ribbon had a light blue central band rather than white as with the standard CGM.*

Granted for 'conspicuous gallantry whilst flying in active operations against the enemy', the CGM (Flying) ranks as one of the rarest gallantry awards. Only 103 were conferred for World War II to the RAF and its New Zealand, Australian and Canadian counterparts and only one after the war (in 1968 to the Royal Australian Air Force for Vietnam).

The detailed citations for some of the WWII awards show just what a remarkable degree of courage was deemed worthy of this decoration. Take for example the award to Flight Sergeant J. M. Hall, 180 Squadron, Royal Air Force, who flew in at least 73 operational sorties; what follows is only a summary of the long recommendation detail.

On the return flight from a bombing raid on the Bocholt railway marshalling yards on the 21st March 1945, a flak shell tore open his Mitchell bomber's cockpit, incapacitating the pilot and severely damaging the aircraft. Having stemmed the flow of blood from his pilot, Dick Perkins, and removed him to the 2nd Pilot's seat, Hall took over the controls of the damaged aircraft. Despite failing pilot training 18 months before, Hall now got a chance to prove his skills under the most testing of circumstances: 'looking at the instrument panel, Hall found he had no airspeed indicator, no rev counter, and no boost gauges working, and the port engine was still giving concern.

*The CGM (Flying) in a group for North West Europe to Flt. Sgt. Hall.*

To add to his problems, the hydraulics were found to be damaged and the bomb doors were hanging down.' He had no working internal intercom and no wireless. Nevertheless, Hall persevered in struggling to control the plane and, overcoming huge odds, he identified a tiny fighter strip, and taking verbal instruction from his seriously wounded pilot, he managed bring the bomber down over the runway and from 50 feet effected a crash landing.

The award was announced in *The London Gazette* of 27th April 1945; Pilot Officer Perkins was awarded the DSO.

As with other medals for gallantry, the CGM (Flying) was rendered obsolete in the reforms of 1993, its place effectively taken by the Conspicuous Gallantry Cross (qv).

*The CGM (Flying) with the AFM – a rare combination.*

# THE GEORGE MEDAL

The George Medal was instituted at the same time as the George Cross (qv) by Royal Warrant of 24th September 1940, published in *The London Gazette* of 31st January 1941. It was essentially an award for acts which were not deemed to reach the standard required of the George Cross but which nevertheless reflected great bravery under difficult and dangerous circumstances.

The medal was created at a time of the mass air bombing of British cities, towns, ports, industrial sites etc. and like the George Cross could be conferred on British and Commonwealth civilian men and women and on police, fire, rescue and civil defence personnel. Members of the armed forces could receive the award for gallantry not in the face of the enemy or in combat (e.g. bomb disposal). The medal is silver and of standard dimensions, with the monarch's

*The George Medal,obverse and reverse of the Elizabeth II type.*

profile and titles current at the time. The reverse, by G. K. Gray, features a fine figure of St. George slaying the Dragon, symbolising the struggle to overcome danger by courage, around which is the wording THE GEORGE MEDAL. Bars were also authorised, these being of the usual flat slip-on laurelled type; no recipient has earned two Bars.

The medal hangs by a simple silver ring suspension from a ribbon of red with five equidistant narrow blue stripes, awards to ladies being worn from a bow fashioned from the ribbon. It is named around the rim in upright serif capitals in a variety of styles, though some military awards are machine impressed and carry the recipient's rank and unit details, as appropriate.

*The first type George Medal in its Royal Mint case of issue.*

Approximately 1,400, with 20 Bars, were awarded for WWII, of which about 720 were conferred on civilians. Many early awards of the GM were made to rescue service personnel and civilians for services during the 'Blitz', in London and elsewhere; all reflect the greatest courage and dedication to duty. As one non-military example, the GM to Police Constable George Taylor for the London 'Blitz' gives a flavour of the type. The award was announced in *The London Gazette* of 9th May 1941 with the following detail:

*The George Medal with second award Bar. Only 27 have so far been awarded.*

'At about 7.45 p.m. 12th November 1940, a high explosive bomb fell at No. 26 Onslow Gardens, Kensington, partly demolishing the house and trapping several people. Police Constable Taylor was off duty in plain clothes, and in the vicinity when the bomb fell. He immediately went to the house, and discovered that the rear had collapsed into the basement. Upon hearing screams, he went to the front part of the basement and assisted two women to safety; he returned and found in another room several Belgian women. These he escorted to other houses, and then informed that the father of one was buried beneath debris in the basement he again returned to the damaged house, obtained the assistance of a soldier and Air Raid Warden, and commenced searching the debris for the victim.

They made their way to the basement, part of which had collapsed under the weight of debris, and regardless of the possibility of a further collapse, pulled away pieces of masonry and brickwork in an endeavour to reach the man, whom they discovered almost completely covered with wreckage.

In the course of this work the constable had to support a large piece of masonry on his back whilst the other two rescuers pulled the wreckage aside. Whilst this was going on they heard somebody walking about in the passage above, and the P.C. shouted a warning that the ceiling would not stand up to the extra strain. It was too late however, as the ceiling suddenly collapsed on top of the rescuers partially burying them, and extinguishing the torch which the P.C. had been holding.

For a moment, Taylor was knocked insensible, but he quickly recovered and found that the soldier had been able to extricate himself but that the Air Raid Warden was apparently still unconscious and partly buried. By making use of water from a broken pipe, P.C. Taylor revived the man, and by using a 'Fireman's lift' carried him to the street, leaving the Warden in the care of A.R.P. personnel. The P.C. then returned to the house, to continue the rescue work, but as he was entering the basement, he suddenly collapsed, and had to be taken to Brompton Hospital by ambulance. He was found to be suffering from concussion, shock and bruised muscles of the back, and had to remain on the sick list for 53 days.'

Awards of the George Medal were made to forces' personnel for services in which military awards would not be appropriate, as illustrated in the award to Gunner Horace Groom, serving in No. 403 Searchlight Battery, Royal Artillery. His GM was announced in *The London Gazette* of 3rd January 1941 with a bland citation, typical of many military awards: 'For conspicuous gallantry in carrying out hazardous work.'

Behind this very non-specific statement lies a much more impressive and gallant story. Groom was serving with his battery at Hucknall in Northants. when, on the night of 23rd/24th September 1940 an aircraft crashed into a house, causing immense damage and starting fires in the area. The 21-year old Gunner Groom ran to the crash site and made four separate rescue attempts, each time bringing an injured child out of the burning debris. During the rescues he was badly burned and was left in a critical condition, though he later recovered.

A rare example of a GM with second award Bar is that to Lieutenant Commander E. D. Woolley, Royal Naval Volunteer Reserve. Having only attended a one day course in mine disposal, he was summoned to deal with a mine in a warehouse on the Thames, for defusing which he gained an immediate GM. After work in many more bomb and mine incidents, including work in the Coventry 'Blitz', he was transferred to Malta in April 1941, where, amidst great secrecy, he won a Bar to his GM for dismantling a captured Italian one-man torpedo craft 'with a complicated firing device'. Woolley remained actively employed in Malta throughout the Island's own 'Blitz', only leaving in September 1943, by which stage he is credited with having rendered safe a total of 30 mines.

*The GM and Bar group to George Woolley.*

In more recent times, the George Medal continues to reward those whose sense of duty and self-sacrifice merits the highest recognition. An example is the GM conferred on a Hong Kong sailor, Chiu Yiu Nam, serving on the Royal Fleet Auxiliary *Sir Galahad* in the Falklands War – one of only three GMs for the South Atlantic campaign.

On 8th June 1982 his ship was bombed by three Argentine Skyhawk jets and, realising that soldiers were trapped inside the burning ship, Chiu donned a protective suit and fought his way time and again through dense smoke and intense flames into the depths of the ship, from where he led injured men to safety; he only obeyed the order to abandon ship when he was sure there was no one left alive. It was only later, after the Commanding Officer of 1st Welsh Guards interviewed surviving guardsmen and heard about their unknown rescuer, that Chiu was identified and his extraordinary gallantry recognised. At least ten men owed their lives to his selfless actions. The Prime Minister, Margaret Thatcher, expressed to Chiu what may be said of so many recipients of gallantry awards – 'your actions are a reminder to us all of the best and noblest aspects of the human spirit'.

*A modern campaign medal group, with George Medal to WO II W. D. Oldham, 321 Explosive Ordnance Disposal Squadron for service in Northern Ireland – for working on the defusing and removal of bombs, serving in 95 incidents.*

To date, about 2,000 George Medals and 27 Bars have been awarded in total, about half of them to military recipients.

# THE INDIAN DISTINGUISHED
# SERVICE MEDAL

Since the Indian Army had its own system of awards, such as the Order of British India and the Order of Merit (qv) established by the East India Company in 1837, Indian soldiers did not receive British gallantry awards like the Distinguished Conduct Medal. As time went by, however, it was felt that another lower-tier decoration was required, since the standard set for the various grades of the Order of Merit was so high. As a result, the Indian Distinguished Service Medal (IDSM) was established in June 1907; it was first awarded for the two North West Frontier campaigns of 1908 but a few early awards were retrospective (e.g. for Waziristan 1901-02).

*The obverse of the scarce Edward VII IDSM; only awarded 1907-1910.*

*The standard reverse of the IDSM, 1907-47. With integral wearing brooch.*

The medal was awarded to all ranks of the native Indian Army and local forces (like frontier militias and levies) and to Indian State forces and was extended in 1917 to non-combatant 'followers', in 1929 to the Royal Indian Marine and in 1940 to the Indian Air Force. The medal was not awarded to Europeans in the Indian service (e.g. officers or corps personnel).

*The slide-on laurelled second award Bar as used on the IDSM and a number of other decorations – like the DCM, MM etc.*

The medal bears on the obverse the profile and titles of the reigning monarch with the simple wording FOR DISTINGUISHED SERVICE on the reverse, surrounded by a wreath of laurel. The Edward VII reverse and first awards of George V had the royal title in Hindi – KAISAR-I-HIND ('Emperor of India') while those issued after c.1933 bore the standard British royal titles. Bars were authorised in June 1917 and take the form of the standard laurelled slip-on types.

*The first type George V IDSM.*

The medals were named in a variety of engraved styles, with machine impressed naming also coming into use during the First World War. The ribbon is dark blue with a central stripe of crimson and attached to a scroll suspension, swivelling until c.1943 when fixed suspensions were adopted. The medal was issued with a laurelled brooch pin for wear.

The IDSM has always been a scarce medal – numerically much rarer than is often supposed. Prior to 1914, only

*The second type George V IDSM with altered titles.*

179, with no Bars, were awarded, with approx. 3,000 and 23 Bars for World War I, approximately 750 and six Bars for interwar campaigns (largely on the North West Frontier) and only 1,200 and 10 Bars for World War II.

Awards were published in *The Gazette of India* and/or *The London Gazette*. Citations for early awards (like the Edward VII version) are very bland, a typical example being 'for recent operations in Waziristan' but later awards can have very detailed citations which reflect great gallantry in action in all the theatres in which the Indian Army was deployed.

*The obverse of the George VI IDSM, with top brooch.*

The Edward VII IDSM in the group shown here was awarded to Subadar Mobin Khan, 59th Scinde Rifles, for his bravery in the Zakka Khel campaign on the North West Frontier in 1908. He was severely wounded in the expedition and his was the first IDSM won by his regiment (conferred per *Governor General's Order* 527 of 1908) and the only one for that campaign. Mobin Khan was also mentioned in despatches for his gallantry in February 1908 in the same campaign (*London Gazette* 22nd May 1908).

*Medal group with Edward VII IDSM, to Subadar Mobin Khan, 59th Scinde Rifles, for gallantry in the Zakka Khel campaign, 1908; with other North West Frontier awards, WWI medals and Delhi Durbar 1911.*

A good WWII example is that to Subadar Amir Khan of 6-13th Frontier Force Rifles, for gallantry in Italy.

> 'From 31st October 1943 to 4th November 1943, during which time the Battalion was in close contact with the enemy in the Tufillo-Mount Farano area, Subadar Amir Khan repeatedly showed outstanding courage in leading the men under difficult circumstances.'

On the night of 3 November, this Subadar was with a detached post from his Company when the enemy put in a counter-attack resulting in close quarter fighting in the dark. The party was surrounded and except for the Subadar and two men all were either killed or captured (a total of 18). Subadar Amir Khan and his two men managed to get into a position on a cliff side where they held on until ordered to withdraw just before daylight. This officer's conduct throughout the actions of Tufillo and Mount Farano was of the highest order and his energy and example inspired and gave added confidence to his men under difficult circumstances.' (*London Gazette* 11th May 1944).

*North West Frontier and WWII campaign group to Subadar Amir Khan, 6-13th Rifles for gallantry in Italy in 1943. With 'mentioned in dispatches' emblems on the India General Service Medal and on the War Medal.*

In total, fewer than 6,000 IDSMs and Bars were ever conferred and as with other Indian Army awards, the medal became obsolete when India achieved independence in 1947.

# THE BURMA GALLANTRY MEDAL

In April 1937, Britain's Burmese possessions were separated from the Indian Empire for administrative purposes. Indian Army awards, like the Order of Merit and the IDSM (qv) were no longer appropriate for what became known as The Burma Army. As a result, and after the beginning of World War II, a new specifically Burmese gallantry award was introduced in the form of the Burma Gallantry Medal (BGM).

Instituted on 10th May 1940, the BGM was intended to reward native Burmese officers and Other Ranks in the Burma Army – some of whom were actually Indians – the Frontier Force and local levies, the Burma Military Police, the Burma Royal Naval Volunteer Reserve and Burma Auxiliary Air Force. Awards to officer ranks ceased in 1945. Notifications of award were published in *The London Gazette* and/or *The Burma Gazette*, with a few appearing in *The Gazette of India*.

*The obverse and reverse of the very rare Burma Gallantry Medal.*

The circular silver medal bore, as usual, the profile and titles of the reigning monarch – only issued with George VI in this case, in the pre-1937 'Indiae Imp.' version; the reverse simply had a laurel wreath with BURMA at the top and FOR GALLANTRY in the centre. The ribbon is 'jungle green' with a central crimson stripe.

The BGM was seldom conferred – 207 medals with only 3 Bars being awarded in total – and many given for service actually behind Japanese lines during the Burma and Far East campaign. Unsurprisingly, given its short life span and low award numbers, examples of the BGM are rarely seen and are consequently very valuable.

An example of the type is that awarded to Subadar Sare Hpung of the war-raised North Kachin Levies – one of a number of tribal levies raised by the British to operate behind enemy lines, utilising their local topographical knowledge.

> 'During the period 16th May to 15th August 1944 this Officer has been responsible for organising or personally commanding platoons of his Company who have ambushed Jap columns on eight separate occasions. On the 10th, 12th, and

*The BGM group to Subadar Sare Hpung, Northern Kachin Levies.*

16th July 44 respectively his men killed a total of 30 Japs. On 20th July 44 his command took 2 Jap prisoners. On the 9th August he again ambushed a party of Japs, killing 2 and wounding others. On the 11th August he was responsible for the capture of 2 Japs and 20 Jap women all attempting to make their way south from Myitkyina. This Officer has off and on commanded his Company and has always set a very high standard by personal example of courage and devotion to duty.' (*London Gazette* 28th June 1945)

Another citation, for the BGM awarded to Lance Naik Aung Thein of the Burma Rifles, illustrates the hardships suffered by those who operated behind enemy lines and the extraordinary degree of determination and loyalty they often displayed:

'He served from August 1942 until September 1942 when he was lost in action on [mount] Bhopi Vum. He underwent long periods of hardship living in close proximity to the enemy, in constant danger and without respite, often short of rations and doing long marches in difficult enemy occupied country with heavy loads. In spite of all this he was always cheerful and showed much courage and initiative in every emergency. He contributed much to the success that has been achieved in providing intelligence regarding enemy movements and dispositions.' (*London Gazette* 19th July 1945)

With the independence of Burma in January 1948, and Burma's withdrawal from the Commonwealth, the medal became obsolete.

# THE DISTINGUISHED SERVICE MEDAL

Apart from the Victoria Cross (qv) and the high-ranking Conspicuous Gallantry Medal (qv) there was in 1914 no decoration available to reward the lower ranks of the Royal Navy for gallantry in action. The new Distinguished Service Medal (DSM) was instituted by Order of Council in October 1914, at a time when it was expected that, since Britain was predominantly a naval power, her war effort would be largely naval. The DSM was intended to reward the Other Ranks of the Royal Navy serving afloat or ashore, and was extended in 1940 to personnel of the RAF serving with the navy and in 1942 to the Merchant Navy and to Army personnel serving afloat (e.g. as gunners on armed merchant vessels).

The silver medal was of standard size and format, with the profile and titles of King George V (in Admiral's uniform) on

*The obverse of the George V DSM. The King in Admiral's uniform.*

*The standard reverse of the DSM. With wearing pin at top.*

the obverse, or of the reigning monarch in subsequent years, and the wording FOR DISTINGUISHED SERVICE enclosed in a wreath of laurel, below a crown on the reverse. Bars for further awards were authorised from June 1916. The medal hung via a straight bar suspension, swivelling until 1941 when fixed, from a ribbon of dark blue with two central white stripes. Awards for 1914-18 service were generally impressed in serif capitals with the recipient's number, initials, surname, rate and name of ship and often bore the date and place of the operation for which the medal was awarded (e.g. 'HMS *Stork* 1917', 'Belgian Coast. 1917', 'Gallipoli Opns. 1915-6'). Post – WWI awards do not carry dates and locational details and later issues were machine impressed.

A fine example of the award of the DSM for an action in the oldest traditions of the Royal Navy is that awarded to Leading Seaman A. S. Fletcher, Royal Naval Reserve, who was decorated for his gallantry during the famous 'ship-to-ship' action between the British armed merchant cruiser *Carmania* and the German armed liner *Cap Trafalgar*, off Trinidad in September 1914. The published heading for the awards in *The London Gazette* of 10th April 1915 is typically brief: 'For services in the action between the *Carmania* and the *Cap Trafalgar*, 14th September, 1914.'

At the outbreak of hostilities in August 1914, the *Cap Trafalgar* was patrolling in South American waters. On the morning of 4th September, off the western end of Trinidad, she was surprised in the act of coaling by the British armed merchant cruiser and ex-liner *Carmania,* under Captain N. Grant, R.N. She attempted to make off at speed but later turned about and prepared to engage. Both ships began firing at 7,500 yards, the 4.7" guns of the *Carmania* doing great damage. The fire from the *Cap Trafalgar* was at first too high, but as the ships closed she began to score, setting the *Carmania* on fire under the bridge and cutting her main water pipe so that the fires could not be brought under control. After an engagement lasting one hour and 40 minutes the *Cap Trafalgar* was heavily on fire and sinking and, despite making a late attempt to disengage and make away, her engines were not equal to the strain and she finally capsized and sank.

The fierceness of the encounter may be judged from the fact that the *Carmania* was hit 79 times and sustained casualties of nine killed and 26 wounded; all her navigational instruments and communicating gear were destroyed, so that she had to be escorted to port in a battered condition. This battle between two closely matched armed liners proved to be the war's longest 'single ship action', more typical of the age of Nelson than of the 'Great War' which was to develop.

*DSM with 1914-15 'trio' to Petty Officer G. Rowe, gun-layer on the Tigris gunboat* **Shaitan** *when she single-handedly captured the town of Amara.*

*DSM (Harwich destroyers) and Sea Gallantry group, with three foreign awards, to Petty Officer F. S. Nicoll – a unique combination.*

The group shown above is that to Able Seaman F. S. Nicoll, who in his WWI career received not only the DSM (left) but also the Sea Gallantry Medal and three gazetted foreign awards – a unique achievement. His DSM was announced in *The London Gazette* of 14th September 1917. Nicoll was serving on the cruiser HMS *Sharpshooter,* part of Admiral Tyrrwhitt's very active Harwich Force. On 5th June 1917 ships of the 5th light Cruiser Squadron bombarded Ostend but were attacked by German destroyers. *Sharpshooter* and the other destroyers drove them off, sinking one and damaging another. For this action Nicoll was awarded the DSM.

Despite the size of Britain's warship fleet and the global range of its activities (in what was after all a world war), the DSM for 1914-18 is rather scarce with only about 4,500, including Bars, being awarded. The figure is much larger for World War II with 7,200 medals and Bars, reflecting the larger scale of actual naval combat and convoy duties, but fewer than 50 after 1945.

*A WWII group, with Atlantic and Italy Stars, showing the DSM and Bar.*

During World War II, when many more DSMs were awarded than in World War I, many fine examples of gallantry which led to the award of the DSM may be found, often earned under the most difficult circumstances of sea and weather.

One such was that to Stoker J. J. Colley, serving on HMS *Achates*. His DSM was announced in *The London Gazette* of 27th April 1943, which simply recounted that it was for 'bravery in Northern waters.' But the story, is of course, much more complicated than that. On 31st December 1942, *Achates* was an escort protecting a convoy en route to Murmansk when she was sunk in the icy waters of the Barents Sea. The German heavy cruiser *Admiral Hipper*, the pocket battleship *Lützow* and six large destroyers had been ordered to attack and destroy the convoy. Despite being heavily outgunned, the escort, under the command of Captain R. St. Vincent Sherbrooke in *Onslow* (subsequently awarded the Victoria Cross), beat off the attack and not one merchant vessel was lost.

*The obverse of the first type George VI DSM (1937-47).*

During the action, *Achates* was hit by gunfire from *Admiral Hipper*, killing the commanding officer and forty crewmen. Despite having sustained severe damage in the shelling, *Achates* continued her work of laying a smoke screen. However, so badly damaged was she that at 13.30 she sank 135 miles ESE of Bear Island, with the loss of 113 seamen; 81 were rescued. The recommendation for Colley stated that:

> 'This man showed remarkable coolness in action, and carried out his duties in the engine room in a calm and most efficient manner. On being ordered to abandon ship he assisted a wounded shipmate out of the engine room on to the upper deck and subsequently got him on to a Carley Float. Throughout he displayed great cheerfulness and in spite of the cold and semi-darkness led community singing while waiting to be picked up.'

Chief Petty Officer H. W. Robinson, Royal Navy – who had already been awarded the George Medal for throwing overboard live ammunition from a burning transport in

Liverpool in 1941 – was awarded the DSM per *London Gazette* of 1st November 1949. This was one of only six DSMs awarded to the Royal Navy for the famous 'Yangtze Incident' in 1949 – two each to HMS *Amethyst, Consort* and *London*. Robinson was serving on *Consort* at the time of the incident.

*The Second World War Coastal Forces DSM group awarded to Motor Mechanic R. L. Capindale, Royal Navy, who 'saved the day' in getting M.T.B. 266 clear of enemy fire in a hotly-contested action off Cape Zebib on the night of 31 March 1943.*

The brief original recommendation states:

> 'For gallantry, dauntless courage, leadership and outstanding devotion to duty under fire. He showed an exceptionally offensive spirit, and set a splendid example to the gun's crews and supply parties. With unfailing energy and dauntless courage, he went wherever trouble occurred, keeping the guns in action despite frequent damage and casualties to the armament and men.'

The confidential report submitted by the Commanding Officer of *Consort*, Commander Ian Robertson, DSC, places Robinson at the top of the list of seventeen officers and ratings specially recommended for gallantry following the Yangtze Incident, stating:

'Of the ratings I should like in particular to mention the conduct of the Gunnery Instructor, Petty Officer Henry William Robinson, who was quite outstanding in setting an example of the offensive spirit to the gun's crews and supply parties, speeding up the latter considerably. Also for his technical skill in dealing with breakdowns at the bofors. In general he displayed the highest qualities of leadership and gallantry (and unselfishness) even to the extent of hurling his false teeth at "those bloody communists!"'

*The 1982 'Defence of South Georgia' DSM group of five awarded to Colour-Sergeant P. J. Leach, Royal Marines, one of just 22 men who held off the Argentine assault on King Edward Point for more than two hours.*

The DSM medal became obsolete in 1993 following reform of the honours system when the DSC (qv) was made available to all ranks as a naval reward.

# THE MILITARY MEDAL

By 1916, the reality of static trench warfare on the Western Front and the serious nature of the fighting in other areas – like Mesopotamia and East Africa – made apparent the need for a lower-tier decoration, ranking below the Distinguished Conduct Medal, to reward acts of gallantry which were regularly being performed on all fronts.

The result was the institution on 25th March 1916 of the Military Medal (MM), announced in *The London Gazette* of 5th April. It was to be awarded to the Other Ranks of the Army, Colonial forces and (from 1944) the Indian Army. Awards were also made to personnel of the Royal Marines, Royal Navy and air forces on occasion, when serving in or in support of land operations. Women were eligible for the MM from June 1916, the awards typically going to nurses who had served under fire, but examples are rare and very valuable. Foreign nationals associated with the British service could also receive the medal, though these were not usually named. All awards,

*The Military Medal, George V, 1st type, obverse and reverse, as awarded in WWI.*

generally excluding those to foreign recipients, are announced in *The London Gazette* and/or other official publications.

The circular silver medal bore on the obverse the profile and titles of the monarch, George V being portrayed in Field Marshal's uniform in the first issue of 1916-36. A 'crowned head' version was issued only between 1930-36, largely awarded for service in Palestine and on the North West Frontier of India, and is very rare. Bars could be awarded for subsequent acts of gallantry; these are of the plain 'laurelled' type which slip over the ribbon and may be stitched down.

*A multiple gallantry group for World War I – the MM with DCM.*

*A World War I MM group, with awards of the French and Belgian **Croix-de-Guerre**.*

The medals were all issued named around the rim in a variety of styles – usually in impressed block capitals or, in the case of some Indian awards for 1944-45, in engraved styles. The ribbon was dark blue with three white and two crimson stripes.

During World War I, approximately 116,000 medals were awarded, with approximately 6,000 Bars. The largest number of Bars awarded was three – of which only one example is known, a remarkable testimony to personal gallantry.

Citations for the MM for 1914-18, detailing the action for which the award was made, are not common. Many recipients seem to have been given a brief typed account of their action,

*The MM with second award Bar and with 1914-15 'trio'. Approximately 6,000 Bars were awarded.*

*An example of the very rare MM with two additional award Bars – only 180 were conferred. With 1914 Star, British War and Victory Medals.*

but few of these papers have survived, even in family hands, and no official record of the recommendations or citations was retained after the war. That for Corporal W. S. Flowers, 2/5th Gloucesters, does survive and suggests the sort of gallantry that could be required to earn the Military Medal:

> 'For especial bravery and a fearless example of devotion to duty in the attack on Robecq on April 23rd 1918. In the absence of the Platoon Sgt., he took command of the front line troops in the attack and in the work of consolidation on gaining the objective. Amidst a devastating rain of enemy shells on the captured position, he was foremost in coolly visiting the company front, cheering the men by his fearless example. On several occasions he exposed himself to enemy sniper fire in order to visit wounded men in other posts and his devotion to duty amounted to courage of a very high order and was instrumental in ensuring the safety of wounded men who would not otherwise have been evacuated owing to their exposed position.'

The award was announced in April 1918; one suspects that earlier in the war, such actions might have earned the DCM!

In the interwar years, something like 300 MMs were awarded, mainly for campaigns in Iraq and Kurdistan, on the North West Frontier of India or in Palestine. World War Two naturally produced a large number of awards, but on nothing like the scale of World War I, with approximately 15,200 medals and 166 Bars conferred; only two were awarded with two Bars. The medal was extended to the Indian Army in 1944 as a lower-tier award ranking below the Indian Distinguished Service Medal (qv) and most of these were given for gallantry in Italy, Burma and the Far East.

*The rare 2nd type ('crowned head') obverse of George V, only awarded between c. 1930-39 – in this case for Palestine.*

*A George VI 1st type MM (with Indiae Imp. title) in a group; awarded for service in Waziristan in 1937.*

Citations or recommendations are more easily available for World War II awards, since they seem to have been officially archived, and are often very detailed – the level of gallantry required to earn the MM in World War II and after was quite impressive! One example for World War II is that awarded to Private C. J. E. Oldridge of the 2nd Devon Regiment, announced in *The London Gazette* of 28th September 1944 with the simple heading 'In recognition of gallant and distinguished services in Normandy.' However, the actual recommendation for the award gives far greater detail for this D-Day award:

> 'At Ryes, during the advance of 2 Devon on 6th June 1944, Private Oldridge was manning a light machine gun in the right forward platoon of the leading company which had been held up by light machine gun and mortar fire. An enemy counter-attack developed on the right flank of the company, and Private Oldridge's platoon was ordered to re-adjust its position to deal with this attack. Private Oldridge remained with his gun in the original position, and, although severely wounded in both legs and both arms by a grenade, successfully broke up the counter-attack, thus preventing the enemy from rushing

the company's position while re-organising. The gallantry and devotion to duty of this man undoubtedly restored the situation, and enabled his company soon to resume the offensive.'

*A George VI MM group with second award Bar to a South African recipient.*

The post-war operations and the 'retreat from Empire' in the 1950s and 1960s saw varying numbers of awards, reflecting the scale of the campaigns. The Korean War saw just over 200 conferred, while the long-drawn-out anti-Communist operations in Malaya (1948-60) resulted in 267 awards of both the

*A Korean War MM group, with the George VI MM, 2nd type, with Indiae Imp. removed, following Indian independence in 1947. The later Korean War MMs were also awarded with the profile of Elizabeth II.*

George VI and Elizabeth II types. Smaller campaigns produced proportionately smaller numbers of awards, all of which are rare and valuable. Examples are those for Aden (19), Borneo (35), the 'Mau Mau rebellion' in Kenya (12), the Suez Crisis (7) and Radfan (6), with 32 conferred for the Falklands War of 1982 and smaller numbers in recent operations in the Balkans, Iraq and Afghanistan. An unusual series of awards of the MM was the 47 conferred on

*An EIIR Military Medal awarded to a Gurkha for service in Malaya.*

Australian personnel for service in the Vietnam War between 1966-69; these are exceptionally rare and examples seldom seen.

The MM continued to be awarded up to the reform of the honours system in 1993, when it was abolished, along with other 'medals' for gallantry. It was largely replaced by the Military Cross, which was then made available to all ranks.

*The posthumous Falklands MM group awarded to Lance-Corporal G. D. 'Gaz' Bingley, The Parachute Regiment, killed in action while leading an attack on an Argentine machine-gun bunker at the Battle of Goose Green, 28 May 1982.*

# THE DISTINGUISHED FLYING MEDAL

Prior to the formation of the Royal Air Force, personnel of Britain's aerial forces had received gallantry awards appropriate to their service – army decorations, like the MC and MM, to the Royal Flying Corps and naval awards, like the DSC and DSM, to the Royal Naval Air Service. When the two services were amalgamated in April 1918 to create the RAF, it was felt that there should be awards which were specific to the new service.

One result of this was the creation of the Distinguished Flying Medal (DFM) by Royal Warrant and *London Gazette* of 3rd June 1918. The new award was granted to the Other Ranks of the RAF for gallantry in the air, 'for an act or acts of valour,

*The George V DFM, obverse and reverse, with second type diagonal striped ribbon.*

courage or devotion to duty performed while flying on active operations against the enemy'.

The silver medal was rather unusual in the British series for being oval in shape. It bore on its obverse the usual effigy and titles of the reigning monarch, within a thin laurel band. A rare 'crowned head' obverse was in use between between 1930-36, with only 22 being awarded. Its reverse, designed by Edward Carter Preston, was much more elaborate and decorative than those of most other British gallantry awards. It featured the figure of the goddess Athena as a *Nike* ('winged Victory') seated on an aeroplane, with a hawk rising from her right hand, above the words FOR COURAGE. The date 1918 was added to the top left of the design in 1938, to commemorate the year of institution. The whole is encircled by a narrow wreath of laurel. Bars were authorised in the original Warrant and take the form of plain slip-on types, with the RAF eagle motif in the centre. Only one DFM was ever awarded with two Bars – to Flight Sgt. D. E. Kingaby, RAFVR, who also received the DSO and AFC during his career.

The ribbon, which hangs from a fixed suspension taking the form of feathered wings, originally comprised alternating thin horizontal stripes of violet and white, but this was quickly altered (in June 1919) to left-right diagonal stripes in those colours. The medal was named in large impressed serif capitals for WWI awards, but for WWII in plain engraved capitals in a variety of styles which, because of the rounded rim of the medal, are often rather crude looking.

The DFM was the Other Ranks equivalent of the officers' Distinguished Flying Cross (qv) and could be awarded to Dominion and Colonial personnel. Because of its late appearance in WWI, it was awarded only in small numbers, so that examples are rare, with approx. 104 and 2 Bars being issued. It was awarded in small numbers for interwar operations (e.g. in Iraq or on the North West Frontier of India) but during World War II, when air operations assumed a much more prominent role, approx. 6,700 DFMs and 61 Bars were conferred.

An example of a First World War award – all of them naturally late in the war – is that to Sgt. Observer A. Newland, RAF, who also received one of only two Bars to the DFM awarded for World War I. The initial award appeared, with typically brief citation, in *The London Gazette* of 21st September 1918:

> 'He is an excellent shot, and has done remarkably well as an observer, gaining the confidence of the pilots with whom he has served. He has personally assisted in shooting down five enemy aeroplanes.'

His Bar was announced in *The London Gazette* of 3rd December 1918:

> 'This non-commissioned officer sets a splendid example of courage, skill and determination to the other non-commissioned officers of his squadron. During the month of August, he crashed six enemy machines.'

These citations mask a remarkable career as an 'Ace', a status he achieved in under a fortnight, being finally credited with 18 enemy aircraft destroyed, one shared and three forced down out of control. On five separate occasions he shot down two aircraft in one air combat, and managed another three in one dogfight. Just one Combat Report (from 31st May 1918) gives a flavour of Newland's ability :

> 'While on Offensive Patrol with 9 Bristol Fighters, 15 E.A. [Enemy Aircraft] were attacked S.W. of Armentieres. Bristol Fighter B1122 (Pilot – Lieut. P. T. Iaccaci. Observer – A.M. A. Newland) saw another of the formation diving down on one Pfalz Scout. 5 Albatross Scouts then dived on the Bristol Fighter. Lt. Iaccaci went down to the assistance of the Bristol Fighter and succeeded in driving the E.A. off. At this time several more E.A. attack them. The Observer (Air Mechanic Newland) put about a drum into a Pfalz Scout and it burst into flames and, after gliding a moment, went out of control and crashed just E.

of Merville. The Observer then put a full drum into an Albatros Scout and it went into a vertical dive, flattening out just before crashing on the Canal Bank S. of Merville. Both machines were fired at about 150 yds. distance.'

During World War II, with its greater employment of aerial forces over a long period, many DFMs were conferred as 'periodic awards' for dedicated service over a series of 'missions', like that awarded to Flight Sgt. C. Allsop. His DFM, announced in *The London Gazette* of 15th August 1944, recorded that:

'This Navigator has operated on 28 occasions, many of them being against heavily defended and distant targets, including eight attacks on Berlin, and two attacks on Leipzig. His steadiness on all occasions and his consistent track keeping were among the main factors which enabled his crew to complete their sorties in safety, and which enabled accurate bombing to be made without dangerous preliminary manoeuvres.'

Other more specific awards reflected exceptional gallantry in the air. That to Sgt. S. Scott (DFM announced in *The London Gazette* 9th January 1945) is just one example:

'A Flight Engineer in a Halifax bomber, Sergeant Scott has taken part in a large number of raids on heavily defended targets, such as Essen, Hamburg, Kiel, Cologne, Nuremberg, Sterkrade, Stuttgart and Duisburg. Sergeant Scott has exhibited, at all times, a great devotion to duty and a thorough knowledge of his trade. Especially was this in evidence when, in April 1943, the crew of which Sergeant Scott was Flight Engineer, were detailed to bomb the Krupps Works at Essen, Germany. On the run in to the target, the aircraft was riddled with flak and five members of the crew were wounded. Despite this, the target was reached and bombed successfully. Sergeant Scott despite a wound which kept him in hospital for eight months, persisted in attending to the fuel supply in the tanks as well as checking the gauges, thus enabling the crippled aircraft to make a landing at an English aerodrome. His indomitable courage and tenacity of purpose in the face of suffering and stress were largely responsible for the safety of the remainder of his crew. His courageous actions are highly commendable.'

Of the awards for World War II, about 170 DFMs and 2 Bars were given as 'honorary' awards to aircrew from non-Commonwealth countries – to American, Polish, French, Czechoslovakian, Dutch, Norwegian, Russian and Belgian recipients.

*A DFC with WWII campaign awards as awarded to a recipient in Bomber Command.*

In the period after 1946, approximately 142 DFMs were awarded – a small number considering the range of conflicts. There were 28 awards for the Korean War, 42 for Malaya 1948-60 and small numbers for the post-imperial campaigns then being waged.

Along with other 'medals' for gallantry, the DFM was rendered obsolete in the honours reforms of 1993, when the DFC (qv) was made available to all ranks.

*The obverse of the EIIR DFM which features the 'uncrowned head' of the monarch.*

*A DFM group for Malaya to the Fleet Air Arm, with Naval General Service for Palestine 1945-48 and General Service Medal for Malaya.*

# THE AIR FORCE MEDAL

The Air Force Medal (AFM) was one of four awards created in June 1918 following the formation of the Royal Air Force in April; the others were the DFC, the DFM and the AFC. (qv)

The new medal was the NCOs and Other Ranks' equivalent of the Air Force Cross and was awarded for gallantry or meritorious service in the air but not generally on active operations or 'in the face of the enemy'. It was granted to British and Commonwealth personnel and honorary awards could be made to foreign recipients.

Like the DFM (qv) the AFM was an oval silver medal with a thin laurel border, bearing on the obverse the profile and titles of the monarch; the reverse carried a depiction of Hermes

*The Air Force Medal, George V obverse and reverse, with later diagonally striped ribbon.*

mounted on a hawk, proffering a wreath – a smaller version of which appears in the centre of the AFC. The date of institution 1918 was added to the reverse in 1938. The medal suspension takes the form of a pair of wings. As with the AFC, the ribbon was originally thin horizontal stripes of red and white but this was altered in July 1919 to left-right diagonal stripes of those colours. Bars, of standard slip-on type with RAF eagle motif to the centre, were authorised for further services.

Only approximately 100 Medals and two Bars were awarded for World War I, with 106 Medals and three Bars during the interwar period. A rare 'crowned head' obverse was used between c. 1930 and 1938. For

*The George V AFM, with original horizontally striped ribbon and the very rare second award Bar.*

service during World War II 259 medals, but no Bars, were conferred and fourteen 'honorary' awards were made to non-Commonwealth aircrew. Civilians were made eligible for the AFM in 1919 but this seems to have been discontinued by 1932, with only three such awards being made.

A fairly typical example of the requirement for the award is shown by the rare interwar AFM conferred on Flight Sgt. (Pilot) B. Crane. Announced in *The London Gazette* of 3rd June 1929, the original recommendation states:

> 'This man is an exceptional pilot and possesses in addition to his flying ability, the power of imparting his knowledge and confidence to his pupils. His total of flying hours exceeds that of any other instructor at the Central Flying School, where he is stationed, and his steadiness, enthusiasm and general example have helped in no small measure to maintain the standards at the School.'

*AFM and medal group to Flight Sgt. B. Crane, including the rare India General Service Medal with clasp 'Waziristan 1925' and RAF Long Service and Good Conduct Medal (far right).*

Some were for much more specific acts, an outstanding example being that awarded to Flight Sgt. J. D. Muir. The award, published in *The London Gazette* of 19th February 1943, included a detailed account:

'One night in December 1942, Sgt. Muir was the pilot of a Wellington aircraft participating in a photo flash bombing exercise. One photo flash was released successfully and the second was about to be released when it exploded in the flare chute and killed the wireless operator. The aircraft became uncontrollable and a fire was started. Sergeant Muir being unable to maintain height, ordered the remaining crew to escape by parachute. This they did with the exception of the navigator who went to the rear of the aircraft to ascertain the precise condition of the wireless operator. After reporting to Sergeant Muir that he could not detect any pulse the navigator then left the aircraft. Sergeant Muir knew that a crash was inevitable but realising that the bomber was in the vicinity of two villages and being uncertain whether the wireless operator was alive or dead, he decided to remain in the aircraft in an endeavour to land clear of the villages. He succeeded in landing the bomber in a field. Sergeant Muir extricated himself just before the aircraft became enveloped in flames, but he was unable to release the wireless operator. Sergeant Muir displayed a high standard of courage and devotion to duty throughout this hazardous experience.'

As might be expected, only small numbers were awarded after the war – including 10 for the Berlin Airlift – with just a few specific to 'end of empire' operations like those in Malaya, Borneo, Cyprus etc. About 500 awards in total were made after 1945, giving a total issue since its introduction in 1918 of fewer than 1,000 medals and 10 second-award Bars. Following the reforms of 1993, the AFM was discontinued and replaced by the AFC, now open to all ranks.

*The obverse of the EIIR Air Force Medal.*

# THE QUEEN'S GALLANTRY MEDAL

The Queen's Gallantry Medal (QGM) was instituted on 20th June 1974 and replaced the British Empire Medal for Gallantry (qv). The circular silver medal, of standard dimensions, features on its obverse the crowned profile of Queen Elizabeth II with the usual titles, while the reverse has THE QUEEN'S GALLANTRY MEDAL in the centre, below a large crown, flanked by sprays of laurel. The medal hangs via a simple ring from a ribbon of dark blue with a thin central stripe of red, flanked by wider stripes of silver-grey. It can be awarded to civil or military personnel, the latter in circumstances generally not 'in the face of the enemy' but for gallantry in saving life and the medal is also awarded to members of the police, fire and rescue services. The recipient's details are impressed around the rim.

*Obverse of the QGM.*　　　　　*Reverse of the QGM.*

One example of the military award of the QGM was that to Corporal Charles Tait of the Duke of Wellington's Regiment, for bravery on duty in Northern Ireland in 1980. Corporal Tait was posted to do duty in a truck leaving Springfield Road Police Station, heading for the military base in Flax Street Mill, his role being to sit in the rear of the truck as an armed rear gunner. As the truck left the protective metal gates of the police station, a group of terrorists, known as the Ballymurphy Gun Team, opened fire with a machine gun at fairly close range from a house backing on to the station. The cab was hit by a number of bullets, severely wounding the driver and a ricochet also hit Corporal Tait in the arm.

*QGM in group for Northern Ireland and with UN medal for Cyprus.*

Unaware that he had been wounded, Corporal Tait immediately left the rear of the truck and ran around to the driver's door. He lifted the driver out of the cab and administered first aid for a face wound that had injured the driver's jaw, causing breathing difficulties. By this time the gunmen had made their escape, pursued by the Quick Reaction Section, and other personnel had come to the aid of the two injured soldiers. Corporal Tait was led away from the scene holding his arm, given first aid and then taken to hospital, from where he made a full recovery and later returned to duty. For his quick-thinking bravery on this occasion, Tait was awarded the QGM, notified in *The London Gazette* of 21st October 1980.

To date, approx. 1,100 QGMs have been awarded, including 19 second award Bars, the most recent being for service in Iraq and Afghanistan. About half of the awards have been earned by military recipients and the rest by civilians and police forces. The Royal Ulster Constabulary has earned the highest total for one service, with approximately 120 awards. 24 have been conferred on women. Posthumous awards were authorised in 1977, 38 so far being granted in this category.

*QGM in group for Northern Ireland and with UN medal for Bosnia and NATO medal for 'Former Yugoslavia'.*

# THE BRITISH EMPIRE MEDAL
# FOR GALLANTRY

In June 1917, the Order of the British Empire was instituted – the last (so far) in Britain's long-established system of Orders. In five classes, more than for any other British Order, it was intended to reward those people in Britain and around the Empire, men and women, who had rendered significant service during 'the Great War' and was retained after the war to become the most commonly-awarded British Order. Original awards reflected achievement in a very wide range of services, professions and institutions – administration, recruiting, training, war production, transport, hospital and nursing, shipping, ordnance and many others. A Military Division was authorised in December 1917, to reward service for which existing military decorations were not appropriate. Civil and Military versions of the insignia were distinguished only by their ribbon – the Military Division had a narrow dark red stripe through the centre of the purple ribbon, while the Civil Division was plain.

*The original 'small size' Medal of the Order of the British Empire (1917-22), with WWI medals as awarded to a female nurse and worn from a ladies' bow.*

Below the five classes of the Order itself, a lower-tier award was created in the form of the Medal of the Order, later known as the British Empire Medal (BEM). Approx. 2,000 of the initial small-type medal were awarded before a design change in 1922, from which time the BEM could be conferred either for meritorious service or for gallantry, the latter being known as the Empire Gallantry Medal (EGM).

*The second type BEM, with 'for gallantry' obverse.*

The obverse of the post-1922 circular silver EGM shows a seated Britannia, with a rising sun in the background, around which is the motto of the Order, FOR GOD AND THE EMPIRE, with FOR GALLANTRY in the exergue in place of MERITORIOUS SERVICE found on the standard type. The reverse had the crowned cypher of George V (GRI) surrounded by six heraldic lions. It is unusual in British terms in not showing the effigy and titles of the reigning monarch. The medal is connected to a plain silver bar suspension by a sprig of laurel leaves.

To visibly distinguish the 'Gallantry' version from the 'Meritorious' type, a silver laurel branch was authorised in 1933, to be worn diagonally across the ribbon. Following the revision of the Statutes of the Order in 1937, the BEM and EGM were altered, redesigning the reverse to show only four heraldic lions and adding the wording INSTITUTED BY KING GEORGE V. At this time, the ribbon was altered to rose pink, with narrow edge stripes of pearl grey, the Military Division having an additional central stripe in pearl grey.

Only 130 EGMs were awarded, about half of them to military personnel who could receive the medal for gallantry in circumstances usually not in combat or in the presence of the enemy – e.g. saving life in an air raid, a criminal incident, a natural disaster, putting out a fire in an ammunition dump etc.

With the introduction of the George Cross and George Medal in 1940 (qv), the EGM ceased to be awarded and recipients (apart from foreign or honorary awards) were asked to exchange the EGM for the George Cross – which some chose not to do.

However, the story of the BEM for gallantry is more complicated than this. The 'meritorious service' version of the medal continued to be awarded and some were actually granted for bravery in World War II (e.g. to Civil Defence or Merchant Navy personnel), where the action was not deemed to fulfil the requirements of the George Cross or George Medal. After 1957, in order to clearly distinguish the award of the BEM for gallantry from that for merit, a silver emblem of crossed oakleaves was worn on the ribbon. The medal could not be awarded posthumously.

One example of the Empire Gallantry Medal (with post-1933 silver laurel branch emblem) is that conferred on Vice Consul Adrian Trapman, serving at Addis Ababa at the time of the Italian invasion of Ethiopia in 1936, published in *The London Gazette* of 1st February 1937:

'Mr. Trapman played a prominent part in the incidents at Abbis Ababa early in May following upon the flight of the Emperor, and was particularly concerned with the rescue of persons from the city, which was in the hands of a disorderly and uncontrolled mob. On the 2nd, 3rd, 4th and 5th May 1936, he took part in expeditions to rescue British and foreign men, women and children from the town to bring them to the safety of the British Legation.

*The BEM with laurel spray emblem for gallantry awarded to Consul Adrian Trapman.*

*The second type BEM, military division ribbon, with gallantry emblem – crossed oakleaves in silver.*

Each expedition involved a drive of some ten miles in an open lorry exposed to dangerous rifle fire from the rioters, many of whom made a practice of discharging their firearms at every passing vehicle.'

A later award, announced in May 1963, gives the flavour of the bravery which could be rewarded with the British Empire Medal for Gallantry (in this case with post-1957 oakleaves). On the 25th November 1962, Trooper Michael E. Downs of the 14/20th King's Hussars and a companion

'were walking along the Promenade at Blackpool when they saw an old man supporting himself by the sea wall. After passing the man they then heard the sound of groaning and splashing coming from the sea. Trooper Downs saw the old man in the water, being carried away from the wall. The tide was fairly high, the sea choppy and there was a heavy swell; it was also very foggy. Trooper Downs, after telling his companion to telephone for assistance and removing some of his clothing, dived into the sea and swam towards the man who was now 50 yards from the sea wall. After a strenuous struggle in the rough water Trooper Downs succeeded in holding the man up with his right hand and started to swim back by breast stroke with his left hand. This was extremely difficult owing to the weight of the man's clothing, but after a great effort he managed to reach the sea wall. Here Trooper Downs dragged the man towards the steps where he was able to pull him almost clear of the water and support him until the arrival of an ambulance. Unfortunately the man died on the way to hospital. Trooper Downs displayed, in the face of forbidding conditions, great gallantry and determination in his efforts to rescue a fellow man.'

He was at that time the youngest military recipient of the award, being only 17 years of age.

The BEM for gallantry, with gallantry emblem, which could not be conferred posthumously, ceased to be awarded after 1974 when the Queen's Gallantry Medal (qv) was instituted. The BEM itself fell victim to the honours reforms of 1993 and was not given to UK recipients (though some Commonwealth awards were made) between then and June 2012 when, on the occasion of the Queen's Diamond Jubilee, it was re-established, though only in its civil division, commonly as a reward for meritorious service over a long period and not for gallantry.

# THE MERITORIOUS SERVICE
# MEDAL FOR GALLANTRY

The Meritorious Service Medal (MSM), introduced as an Army award as long ago as 1845 and first conferred in 1847, was intended to reward exceptionally long service of a distinctly meritorious character. Since most were awarded to long-serving senior NCOs, it was often called 'the Sergeant's Medal' and could be awarded with a variable monetary gratuity. The standard required to earn the medal was high, so pre-1914 awards are rather scarce. MSMs were created for the Royal Marines in 1849 but other services had to wait until the First World War and after to be eligible for their own version of the medal – the RAF in June 1918 and the Royal Navy in January 1919.

*The MSM as awarded for Gallantry during the period 1916-28.*

*The obverse of the George V MSM, the king in Admiral's uniform, as awarded to the Royal Marines and Royal Navy. Worn here with the Royal Navy Long Service and Good Conduct Medal.*

During World War I, it became apparent that many men were contributing to the work of their unit or to the war effort in general 'above and beyond the call of duty' and that some means of rewarding their service should be created. It was therefore decided in 1916 that the MSM should be granted not only for long service, as before, but also as an 'immediate award' for merit to all ranks below officer status in British and Imperial (but not Indian) forces. The 'immediate' awards of the British MSM could be granted for bravery, though not 'in action' – e.g. for dealing with grenade training accidents, fires in ammunition dumps or in arsenals or saving life under dangerous circumstances.

The contemporary Indian Meritorious Service Medal (first established in 1888 as a reward for long and meritorious service, like its British counterpart, but of distinctive design) was also conferred as an 'immediate' award from 1917-1925, rewarding service in many wartime theatres and later on the

*Obverse of the Indian Army MSM. Like the British version, it could be granted as an 'immediate' award for 1914-18 service and some were conferred for gallantry.*

*The distinctive 'lotus flower' reverse of the Indian Army MSM.*

North West Frontier and elsewhere (e.g. Iraq). Some were granted for gallantry, though it is difficult to establish from published official sources. Approximately 5,750 of these war-service 'immediate' types of Indian MSM were issued, with only a handful of Bars known. Citations rarely exist, but regimental histories can sometimes provide extra detail.

The Army MSM 'for gallantry' is no different in design than the standard British long-service version – a circular silver medal bearing on the obverse the titles and effigy of King George V, in Field Marshal's uniform; the reverse has the simple wording FOR MERITORIOUS SERVICE below a crown, surrounded by a wreath of laurel. As usual with British awards, notification of the fact of an award is published in *The London Gazette* and similar official publications; the only way to distinguish a 'gallantry' MSM from the standard version is in the citation (where it exists) or from *The London Gazette* entry which sometimes details the award circumstances.

*The obverse and reverse of the George V MSM, the king in Field Marshal's uniform as awarded to the Army.*

The medal hangs via a scroll suspension from a ribbon of crimson with three narrow white stripes. The recipient's details are machine impressed around the rim, similar to other British medals for World War I.

As with 'immediate' awards of the MSM in general, the use of the 'gallantry' type ceased in 1928, by which time fewer than 450 had been issued, so that they are rarely seen. Similar 'immediate' awards to the Royal Navy and RAF ceased in the same year.

# MENTIONS IN DISPATCHES AND COMMENDATIONS

For generations, it was common for commanding officers to bring forward ('mention') in their official accounts of operations and battles the names of those who had distinguished themselves through bravery or particularly meritorious service. The lists of those 'brought forward' were usually dominated by officers, with NCOs and Other Ranks occurring much more rarely, a 'mention' for them frequently forming the basis for the award of an actual medal like the DCM. The fact of a 'mention' appeared in *The London Gazette* and similar official publications where the campaign was deemed significant enough to merit the dispatches being published in the first place. It was recorded in the 'War Service' records of officers and in the personal papers of Other Ranks in all branches of service. But, whatever the rank, there was no wearable emblem, or any visible indication of the honour.

*An example of a 1914-18 gallantry card. Many (but not all) regiments, brigades and divisions produced their own kind. Recognition in this form was sometimes the precursor of an actual medal award.*

The First World War brought about a change in this system. Since so many men and women in all branches of imperial service had been 'brought to notice' for some action, gallant or otherwise, it was decided to award an actual emblem as a visible token of the fact. The first emblem took the form of a spray of oakleaves in bronze, to be stitched diagonally

*(Left) The mention in dispatches oakleaf emblem.*

*(Below) Ribbon bar showing the smaller MID emblem carried when ribbons alone were being worn.*

across the ribbon of the Victory Medal or, if this had not been awarded, the relevant war or campaign medal. Approximately 140,000 'mentions' were rewarded in this way for World War I and post-war service up to 1920, including British and Imperial service personnel, women, civilians and foreign nationals. The list of recipients rarely gives any detail of the circumstances of award, though it may refer to the theatre of war and the dates covered.

Only one emblem was to be worn no matter how many times the recipient had been 'mentioned' during a war or campaign – and many had several 'mentions'. In August 1920, the emblem was altered to a single bronze oakleaf, pinned through or sewn onto the ribbon of the appropriate

*The bronze 'mention in dispatches' oakleaf spray, introduced at the end of World War One and worn on the ribbon of the Victory Medal.*

135

*Medals for 1914-18 showing the MID emblem. Only one emblem could be worn.*

campaign medal or on the War Medal (only) in the case of World War II awards. Smaller versions are worn on ribbon bars.

The World War II 'Mention' to Stoker Petty Officer AH Binfield is a good example of what such an award might entail. *The London Gazette* of 9th November 1943 recorded that he was 'mentioned' for 'gallant and distinguished service in action with enemy submarines while serving in His Majesty's Ship ... *Balsam'*. The corvette *Balsam* was one of three convoy escorts which attacked an enemy submarine with depth charges.

The original recommendation – which was for a DSM but downgraded – read:

> 'For skill and devotion to duty at his action station as Engine Room Stoker Petty Officer during a successful action against an enemy submarine [U-135]. The maneouvres of the escorts from the time that this U-Boat attacked the convoy at 10.20 until

*(Far Left) The single bronze oakleaf 'mention' emblem introduced in 1920 and worn here on the India General Service Medal, 1936-39.*

*(Left) The single bronze oakleaf 'mention' emblem worn on the ribbon of the War Medal, as for WWII awards.*

*(Below) A DSC group for 1939-45 showing the MID emblem. For WWII, the emblem was only worn on the ribbon of the War Medal.*

its final destruction at 12.06 were such as to call for a high degree of skill and care from the engine room personnel. The operations required of escorts to ensure the destruction of this U-Boat could not have been accomplished without the skill and devotion to duty of the engine room department'.

With the honours reforms of 1993, the single bronze oakleaf was altered to silver and its award criteria were made more specific, so that the emblem is now defined as an actual gallantry award for acts of bravery during active operations. From 2003, in addition to British campaign medals, the MID device can be worn on United Nations, NATO and EU medals and a further change in 2014 decreed that up to three emblems may be worn on a single campaign medal and ribbon Bar for those with multiple mentions, backdated to 1962.

The King's (or Queen's) Commendation for Valuable Service in the Air was introduced in 1942 to reward meritorious or gallant service which fell below the standard required for the Air Force Cross or Air Force Medal. The emblem for service personnel was exactly the same as that for a 'mention in dispatches' – a bronze oak leaf – and could be worn *in addition to* an actual MID emblem in cases where both had been earned, providing the only occasion where two oakleaf MID emblems may be seen on one medal ribbon.

For recipients in civil aviation, the emblem took the form of a small white-metal badge, to be worn below a row of medals or medal ribbons, while the King's or Queen's Commendation for Bravery takes the form of a silver laurel spray worn across the appropriate medal ribbon; this replaced a plastic pin-back badge awarded from 1942-45.

*The original King's Commendation badge, in plastic.*

*Silver laurel emblems for the Queen's Commendation for Bravery, with presentation box.*

The current Queen's Commendation for Bravery in the Air (not in the presence of the enemy) comprises a silver RAF eagle device worn on a medal ribbon, while the Queen's Commendation for Valuable Service takes the form of a silver oakleaf spray. As with the MID oakleaf, these modern emblems may be worn on the ribbons of British, UN, EU or NATO medals.

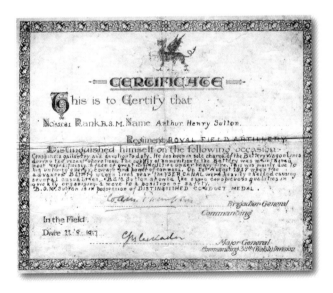

*A 1917 gallantry certificate produced by the 38th Welsh Division.*

# OTHER GALLANTRY AWARDS
# TO THE ARMED FORCES

**The New Zealand Cross** was instituted in 1869 by the New Zealand colonial authorities, to reward exceptional gallantry during the last phase of the Maori Wars (1860-72). It reflected the feeling in the colony that British awards were not an adequate reward to the local units raised during the campaigns and who bore the brunt of the later fighting, especially since the Victoria Cross could not at that time be awarded to colonial militias. The award was frowned upon by the authorities in London, since it was a local initiative without royal sanction and it was eventually suppressed, with only 23 awarded. It constitutes the rarest of the gallantry awards in the British and Imperial series and examples are seldom seen, though finely-made replicas sometimes occur on the market.

*A fine replica of the New Zealand Cross. The originals are excessively rare.*

**The Albert Medal**, named in honour of Prince Albert and instituted in 1866, was initially a high-ranking award for saving life at sea. It was an early example of an *official* national medal to recognise bravery in saving life, existing awards at that time having been conferred only by societies, like the Royal Humane Society, or by the Board of Trade with its Sea Gallantry Medal of 1855 (qv). Extended in 1867 to two classes, gold and bronze, it was opened to land service 1876. The ribbon distinguished sea or land rescues – stripes of blue and white for sea service or red and white for land service. Primarily intended to reward civilians and merchant navy personnel, awards were made to military recipients for service not 'in the presence of the enemy' (e.g. bravery dealing with ammunition fires, as at the Ferozepore Arsenal in 1907). The award was effectively replaced by the George Cross from 1940 and recipients could exchange one for the other, though not all did so. The gold medal was finally abolished in 1949 and the bronze type only given posthumously after that date. The decoration was regarded as obsolete by 1971.

*(Far Left) The Albert Medal for Sea Service. The plain reverse of the medal is engraved with the recipient's name and details of the incident for which the award was made.*

*(Left) The Albert Medal in bronze for Land Service.*

**The Order of British India** (OBI) was established by the Honourable East India Company in 1837, along with the Order of Merit (qv). Essentially, the OBI was a long-service reward for Indian officers but examples are known as special and immediate awards for distinguished service or gallantry on campaign. In two classes, both worn around the neck, the Second Class conferred the title *Bahadur* ('Hero') and the First Class the title *Sardar Bahadur* ('Heroic Leader'); the titles are used, for example, in entries in the Indian Army Lists for the various recipients. Holders had to progress from the lower to the higher class. The Order was not conferred on Europeans and it ceased to be awarded after Indian independence in 1947.

*(Above Right) 1st class of post 1939 type, when the enamel wording was also rendered in light blue enamel and coloured central stripes added to the ribbon to denote class – two stripes for 1st Class and one stripe for the 2nd Class.*

*The Order of British India. 1st Class ('Sardar Bahadur'), 1st type.*

*The Order of British India. 2nd Class ('Bahadur'), 1st type.*

**The Order of Burma**, established in 1940, was essentially the same as Order of British India – i.e. an officer's long-service award – but rewarding Burmese officers of the Burma Army, which was separated from the Indian Army in 1937, when Burma came under separate administration. In only one class, worn as a neck badge, the Order was not conferred on Europeans and it ceased to be awarded after Burmese independence in 1948. It has always been a very rare decoration, with only approximately 24 ever issued.

*Neck Badge of the Order of Burma – a very rare decoration.*

**The Sea Gallantry Medal** was established in 1855 and – most unusually – by Act of Parliament, associated with the Merchant Shipping Act of 1854 and awarded by the Board of Trade. It was originally given as a non-wearable gold, silver or bronze medal but it was transformed into a medal of standardised, wearable form in these metals in 1903. The gold type may never have been issued since no examples have been seen or recorded. Intended largely as a reward to civilians and seafarers (e.g. merchant navy and fishing fleet personnel), it was granted in two types – for 'humanity' in efforts to save life, or for 'gallantry' where the personal risk was greater. Like so many other largely civil awards, it could be awarded to military recipients for rescues at sea not 'in the presence of the enemy' (e.g. rescues at sea or saving life on a sinking troopship). Only one second-award Bar was ever conferred and the medal seems to have fallen into disuse by 1989.

*The Sea Gallantry Medal. Bronze version of the first (non-wearable) type.*

*Sea Gallantry Medal in silver, post 1903 wearable type, with obverse of George V.*

**Society Awards.** There is a large range of local and 'society' medals established to reward gallantry in saving life (e.g. the Liverpool Shipwreck and Humane Society's awards). The most well-known and often seen are those of **the Royal Humane Society.** Founded in 1774, originally to teach emergency resuscitation and life saving, it was concerned with the rescue of those who risked drowning or with rescues at sea and was the first *national* society to award medals for bravery. Branches of the Society were established around the empire (e.g. in Canada) and awarded their own national types. The Society later broadened its remit to include rescues not just at sea but including mining, industry, transport etc. and in the military as well as civil spheres.

*Original non-wearable type of RHS medal in silver.*

*Smaller (post 1869) wearable medal in silver. Reverse.*

*RHS medal in bronze. Obverse. Note the integral buckle brooch bar.*

Its medals were initially awarded in large non-wearable cased or 'table' forms in gold, silver and bronze but in 1869 they were converted to the usual wearable types of standard size (38 mm diameter), suspended from a plain dark blue ribbon via a swivelling scroll suspension. Dated Bars were conferred for subsequent actions. Awards were made for 'successful' or 'unsuccessful' rescue attempts, the Latin wording on the award reflecting this aspect. From 1873, an annual gold medal (in memory of Captain C. S. S. Stanhope) was awarded to the rescue deemed to be the most gallant of that year. It resembled the RHS silver award, but was worked in gold and bore a clasp reading *STANHOPE MEDAL* below the year of award (e.g. *1896*). However, since 1937 the Stanhope Medal has been identical to the other RHS medals, except that it is made of gold. RHS medals are still awarded.

*The Stanhope Medal for 1899; there was only one award per annum.*

# SOME FOREIGN DECORATIONS TO BRITISH PERSONNEL

When British forces have served on campaign alongside allied forces, it has been common for the associated power to confer its own gallantry awards on British personnel. Examples are French and Ottoman awards to British soldiers and sailors in the Crimea 1854-56 and Ottoman awards for Egypt 1882 and for subsequent Egyptian and Sudanese campaigns between 1884-1914.

The neck badge and breast star of the 2nd Class of the Order of the Medjidieh. The ribbon of the order was red with a narrow stripe of green to each edge.

The neck badge and breast star of the 2nd Class of the Order of the Osmanieh. The ribbon of the order was grass green with a narrow red stripe to each edge.

Many different types of orders, decorations and medals from within the existing honours system of a wide range of allied powers have been awarded to British recipients, so that some rare and unusual awards are seen in British groups. Both World Wars in particular provided ample opportunity for the award of decorations by allied powers and it is common to see French, Belgian, Italian, Serbian, Japanese, Russian, American and other foreign awards, as relevant, in medal groups to British and Imperial recipients.

The list below is just a small sample of the more commonly seen foreign awards which have been conferred on British recipients over the years.

The Ottoman (Turkish) Empire awarded a series of orders and decorations to British personnel fighting as allies at various times. A commonly seen Ottoman award is the Order of the Medjidieh (1852) of which many awards were made, in various classes, to British forces for service in the Crimea and in Egypt and the Sudan between 1882-1914. Also seen, though somewhat rarer, are the various grades of the Ottoman Order of the Osmanieh (1862).

As a major ally in the Crimea and in both world wars, France conferred a large number of its own awards on British and other Allied personnel. The prestigious *Legion d'Honneur* (1802) was conferred in various grades, usually but not always on officers, for the Crimean War (1854-56) and both World Wars. The *Medaille Militaire*, introduced in 1852 as a high-ranking decoration originally for Sergeants and Generals in the French service, was widely conferred on British 'Other

*The 4th Class (identified by the ribbon rosette) of the Legion of Honour, WWI period.*

*The original (1852) version of the Medaille Militaire, as awarded to British forces in the Crimea.*

*The republican (post 1871) Medaille Militaire as awarded in the 1914-18 war and after.*

Ranks' during the Crimean War and more especially during World War I. The French *Croix-de-Guerre* (War Cross) was instituted in 1915 and many awarded to British and Imperial forces of all ranks and services. Ribbon emblems denote the level of 'mention' in official dispatches (regimental, brigade, corps etc.) and more than one ribbon emblem could be worn. Other French orders and decorations seen in British medal groups range from rather specialist awards like the Order of Agricultural Merit to colonial Orders like the Black Star of Benin and others.

The bronze Belgian *Croix-de-Guerre*, instituted in October 1915 was, like its French equivalent, widely awarded in both World Wars and could carry a range of ribbon emblems for different services. Also sometimes seen are the various grades of the Order of Leopold, which is frequently seen with the *Croix-de-Guerre*.

*(Left) The French **Croix de Guerre**, 1914-18 period, with bronze palm.*

*(Right) The standard French **Croix-de-Guerre of WWII** period, with bronze star. There are a number of types and varieties.*

*The Belgian **Croix de Guerre** of 1914-18, obverse; with palm, carrying 'A' for King Albert.*

*The Belgian **Croix de Guerre** of 1939-45, obverse, with palm carrying the monogram of Leopold III.*

*The Belgian **Croix de Guerre** of 1939-45, reverse.*

149

The Kingdom of Italy awarded its own orders and decorations to allied forces, though not, of course, for World War II. Most commonly seen of the former are various grades of the Order of the Crown, with its distinctive 'love knot' motif, and of the latter the Italian War Cross (*Croce di Guerra*) and the Medal for Military Valour (*Al Valore Militare*). The bronze War Cross was a wartime production, instituted in 1918 and widely conferred on allied personnel, especially those serving in the north-east Italy theatre. The *Al Valore Militare,* awarded in gold, silver and bronze grades, was a much more old-established decoration, dating to 1833 when founded by the Kingdom of Savoy. Both are still conferred.

*The Order of the Crown, Knight's breast badge.*

*The Italian **Al Valore Militare**, standard obverse, 1914-18 type. The reverse often carries the recipient's name and regimental or unit details.*

*The Italian **Croce di Guerra** (War Cross). Obverse.*

The Kingdom of Serbia conferred a range of attractive orders and decorations which are sometimes found in British medal groups, especially for World War I and in particular for service in the Balkans and on the Salonika front. Amongst the most frequently seen – though none is very common – is the Order of the White Eagle. Seen here are the obverse and reverse of the breast badge, worn from its original ribbon. All Serbian awards for war service 1914-18 were worn from a plain red ribbon and carried crossed swords to signify combatant service. Medals in gold, silver and bronze 'for Zeal' and for bravery are also seen.

*The Serbian Medal for Zeal. They were awarded in 'gold' (gilt), silver and bronze.*

*The attractive breast badge of the Serbian Order of the White Eagle, 5th Class. When awarded for war service 1914-18, all Serbian awards were worn from a plain red ribbon.*

As a major British ally until the fall of the monarchy in the October Revolution of 1917, Tsarist Russian awards are sometimes seen in British medal groups, including some of their exquisite Orders – regarded by many as the finest ever produced in terms of their design and quality. The various grades of the Crosses and Medals of the Order of St. George are frequently seen in British gallantry groups; such awards were made for Ypres 1915 and Jutland in 1916 but ceased to be officially conferred after the fall of the Romanov monarchy in 1917. Some Russian Orders, however, continued to be awarded by monarchist forces to personnel of British and Allied intervention forces during the Russian Civil War (1918-20). They are often of noticeably lower quality, for fairly obvious reasons.

*The Russian Medal of the Order of St George or 'Medal for Bravery'.*

*The 4th Class of the Cross of the Order of St George.*

*The neck badge of the Order of St. Stanislas, 2nd Class. A Czarist Order sometimes seen in British medal groups and typical of the fine quality of Russian insignia. Crossed swords carried on the badge, on the suspension or on the ribbon symbolise war or combatant service and are to be found on the awards of many European countries.*

The United States of America has conferred comparatively few decorations on its allies. Amongst those sometimes seen are the various grades of the Legion of Merit and the Bronze Star. Most US decorations are seen in WWII groups and are rare as such before 1939.

*The Legion of Merit. Unusual in the US series since it is effectively an 'Order', awarded in various grades for meritorious service.*

*The US Bronze Star. Like the Silver Star, an award for gallantry in action and sometimes seen in British medal groups.*

Japanese awards, whose insignia are regarded as some of the finest seen in terms of quality and workmanship, are somewhat rare in British groups, but as an ally before and during WWI, examples of the various grades of the Order of the Rising Sun and the Order of the Sacred Treasure are sometimes found to British recipients.

*(Right) The Order of the Rising Sun, 4th Class. The 'rising sun' takes the form of a beautiful cabochon garnet.*

*(Left) The Order of Sacred Treasure, 3rd Class neck badge; the design features the sword, mirror and necklace of ancient tradition.*

*(Below) A British medal group with a multiplicity of foreign orders and decorations (worn after the British awards, as is standard protocol), including from left to right: Egyptian Order of the Nile, French Legion of Honour, Greek Order of George I, Russian Order of St. Anne and Ottoman Order of Medjidieh.*

# READING LIST

There is a large and growing list of reference books on British, Imperial and Commonwealth gallantry awards.

Despite its age, still the best general introduction is P. E. Abbott and J. M. A. Tamplin, *British Gallantry Awards*, Seaby, 1971 (and expanded in later editions).

Other useful works are :

[n/s] *The Register of the George Cross*, This England, *1990*.

Abbott, P. E., *Recipients of the DCM 1855-1909*, Hayward, 1975.

Bate, C. K., and Smith, M. G. *For Bravery in the Field: the MM 1919-91*, Bayonet Publications, 1991.

Bowyer, Chaz., *For Valour: the Air VCs*, Airlife, 1992.

Brown, G. A., *For Distinguished Conduct in the Field: the DCM 1939-1992*, Western Canadian Distributors, 1993.

Brazier, K., *The Complete George Cross*, Pen and Sword, 2012.

Carter, N. & C. J., *The Distinguished Flying Cross and How it Was Won, 1918-1995*, Savannah, 1998.

Chhina, R. and Parrett, C., *Indian Order Of Merit. Historical Records 1837-1947, Vol. I, 1837-60*, Tom Donovan, 2010.

Chhina, R., *The Indian Distinguished Service Medal*, Invicta India, 2001.

Clarke, J. D., *Gallantry Medals and Awards*, Patrick Stephens, 1993.

Cooper, A. W., *In Action with the Enemy: Holders of the Conspicuous Gallantry Medal (Flying)*, Harper Collins, 1986.

Creagh, Sir O. M., and Humphris, E. M., *The Distinguished Service Order, 1886-1923*, Reprinted by J. B. Hayward, 1978.

Duckers, P., *Reward of Valor: the Indian Order of Merit 1914-18*, Jade Books, 1999.

Duckers, P., *British Gallantry Awards 1855-2000*, Shire Books, 2005 and 2010.

Fevyer, W. H., *The DSC 1901-38,* London Stamp Exchange, 1991.

Fevyer, W. H., *The DSM 1914-1920,* J.B. Hayward, 1982.

Fevyer, W. H., *The DSM 1939-1946*, J.B. Hayward, 1981.

Fevyer, W. H., *The George Medal,* Spink, 1980.

Hearns, D. V. P., *Companions of the Distinguished Service Order 1920-2006,* Naval and Military Press, 2014.

Henderson, D. V., *Heroic Endeavour: Complete Register of the Albert, Edward & Empire Gallantry Medals and How They Were Won,* J. B. Hayward, 1988.

Mackinley, G. A., B*eyond Duty (The DCM to the British Commonwealth 1920-1992),* James Stedman, Sydney, 1993.

Maton, M., *Honour Those Mentioned in the Great War*, 3 vols., Token Publishing, 2011.

Maton, M., *Honour Those Mentioned : The Army, World War Two*, 2 vols., Token Publishing, 2011.

Maton, M., *Honour Those Mentioned: The Navy, World War Two,* Token Publishing, 2012.

Maton, M., *Honour Those Mentioned: The Air Forces, World War Two,* Token Publishing, 2010.

Maton, M., *Honour The Recipients of Foreign Awards,* Token Publishing, 2013.

Maton, M., *Honour The Civilians, World War Two*, Token Publishing, 2012.

Maton, M., *Honour the Officers: Honours and Awards to British,*

*Dominion & Colonial Officers During WWII,* Token Publishing, 2009.

Maton, M., *Honours and Awards and Mentions in Dispatches, 1854-1914 and 1920-1939,* Token Publishing, 2017.

McDermott, P., *Acts of Courage: Register of the George Medal 1940- 2015,* Worcestershire Medal Services, 2016.

McDermott, P., *For Conspicuous Gallantry. The Register Of The Conspicuous Gallantry Medal 1855-1992,* Naval and Military Press, 2009.

McInnes, I., *The Meritorious Service Medal: Immediate Awards 1916-28,* Naval and Military Press, 1992.

Metcalfe, N., *For Exemplary Bravery - The Queen's Gallantry Medal,* N. Metcalfe, 2014.

Peterson, C., *Unparalleled Danger, Unsurpassed Courage - Recipients of the Indian Order of Merit in the Second World War,* N/S, 1997.

Sainsbury, Major J. D., *For Gallantry in the Performance of Military Duty* (the MSM for Gallantry, 1916-28), Samson, 1980.

Richardson, M., *Deeds of Heroes: The Story of the Distinguished Conduct Medal 1854-1993,* Pen and Sword, 2012.

Stanistreet, A., *Heroes of the Albert Medal,* Token Publishing, 2002.

Stanistreet, A., *More Heroes of the Albert Medal,* Token Publishing, 2015.

Tavender, I., *Distinguished Flying Medal: A Record of Courage, 1918-82,* J. B. Hayward, 1990.

Thornton, N., *For Conspicuous Gallantry: Military Cross Heroes of the First World War,* Fonthill Press, 2018.

Walker, R. W., *Recipients of the DCM 1914-20,* Midland Medals, 1981.

Walker, L., *Citations of the Distinguished Conduct Medal*

*1914-1920.* Various volumes, Naval and Military Press, 2007.

Warrington, P., *For Bravery in the Field: British Army Recipients of the Military Medal 1914-20,* Naval and Military Press, 2014.

The Victoria Cross is a subject in itself and there is a large library of specialist reference works dedicated to it. A few examples are :

Carroll, F. G., *The Register of the Victoria Cross,* This England, 1988.

Ashcroft, Michael (Lord), *Victoria Cross Heroes,* Headline Review, 2007.

Ashcroft, Michael (Lord), *George Cross Heroes*, Headline Review, 2007.

Arthur, M., *Symbol of Courage: A Complete History of the Victoria Cross,* Sidgwick & Jackson, 2003.

Bailey, R., *Forgotten Voices of the Victoria Cross*, Ebury Press, 2011.

Bancroft, J. W., *Local Heroes: Boer War VCs,* The House of Heroes, 2003.

Batchelor, P. F., and Matson, C., *VCs of the First World War: The Western Front 1915,* Wrens Park Publishing, 1999.

Best, B., *The Victoria Cross Wars: Battles, Campaigns and Conflicts of All the VC Heroes,* Frontline Books, 2017.

Bowyer, C., *The Air VCs,* Kimber, 1978.

Cooksley, P. G., *VCs of the First World War: the Air VCs,* Wrens Park Publishing, 1999.

Duckers, P., *The Victoria Cross,* Shire Books, 2005.

Gliddon, G., *VCs of the First World War: 1914*, Budding Books, 1997.

Gliddon, G., *VCs of the First World War: the Somme,* Budding Books, 1997.

Gliddon, G., *VCs of the First World War: the Spring Offensive 1918,* Sutton Publishing, 1997.

Gliddon, G., *VCs of the First World War: Arras and Messines 1917,* Wrens Park Publishing, 2000.

Gliddon, G., *VCs of the First World War: The Final Days 1918,* Sutton Publishing, 2000.

Gliddon, G., *VCs of the First World War: The Road to Victory 1918,* Sutton Publishing, 2000.

Kempton, C., *Valour and Gallantry: HEIC and Indian Army VCs and GCs 1856-1946,* The Military Press, 2001.

Laffin, J., *British VCs of World War Two: A Study in Heroism,* Budding Books, 2000.

Little, M. G., *The Royal Marines VCs,* Royal Marines Museum, no date.

Napier, G., *The Sapper VCs,* HMSO, 1999.

Snelling, S., *VCs of the First World War: Gallipoli,* Wrens Park Publishing 1999.

Snelling, S., *VCs of the First World War: Passchendaele,* Sutton Park Publishing 1998.

Turner, J. F., *VCs of the Royal Navy,* George Harrap, 1956.

Turner, J. F., *VCs of the Air,* George Harrap, 1961; reprinted by Wrens Park Publishing 2001.

Turner, J. F., *VCs of the Army 1939-51,* George Harrap, 1962.

Uys, I. S., *VCs of the Anglo-Boer War,* Uys, 2000.

Williams, W. A., *The VCs of Wales and the Welsh Regiments,* Bridge Books, 1984.

Winton, J., *The VC at Sea,* M. Joseph, 1978.

In this day of internet access, a simple Google search on specific medals, regiments or campaigns will raise a wide range of information on any subject or on other sources of information.

Major archives holding both original documents and

published sources whose collections can be searched online include:

The National Archives in Kew (http://www.nationalarchives.gov.uk)

The Imperial War Museum (https://www.iwm.org.uk)

The National Army Museum (https://www.nam.ac.uk)

The India Office collections held in the British Library in Euston (*https://www.bl.uk/collection-guides/india-office-records*)

*The London Gazette* can be searched and consulted online via its website: https://www.thegazette.co.uk

The British Newspaper Archive collection of online newspapers is of great value: http://www.britishnewspaperarchive.co.uk

Local archives and reference libraries and local regimental and military museums may also offer good sources of information, some of which are searchable online via the *Access2Archives* database at the National Archives.

See also the Army Museums Ogilby Trust website at www.armymuseums.co.uk for a definitive listing of British regimental museums and their websites, and directions to a large range of military reference books and helpful sites.

The National Archives of Canada, New Zealand and Australia also have good searchable online sites.

# INDEX